Chain / 1

Special Topic: Gender And Editing

Edited by Jena Osman and Juliana Spahr

Chain
Spring/Summer 1994

Editors: Jena Osman and Juliana Spahr

Typesetting and Design: Kristin Prevallet

Cover Art and Interior Figures: AnJanette Brush

Subscriptions: *Chain* appears annually. Send orders to *Chain* at
107 14th St., Buffalo, NY 14213. Make checks payable to UB
Foundation. $7.95 for one issue, $14.00 for two.

This issue was made possible by the Samuel P. Capen Chair of
Poetry and Humanities (Robert Creeley), the David Gray
Chair of Poetry and Letters (Charles Bernstein), the James H.
McNulty Chair (Dennis Tedlock), the Graduate Student
Association, the Mother Language Association, and
Sub-board I, all of the State University of New York at Buffalo.

ISSN 1076-0520
ISBN 0-922668-12-4

Contents

Editorial Forum

Dear Editor,

We are currently soliciting work for a new journal called *Chain*, devoted to the work of women poets, editors and critics. The journal will consist of two parts: a critical forum on editorial practices and a series of "chains"/poems and other responses that enact an alternative editorial practice.

We would like to hear from you about your experiences as an editor. Please consider the following questions and/or issues:

- How has editing influenced your other work?
- Does gender play a role in your editorial practice?
- Editing as power or subversion of it
- What obligations do you answer to as an editor?
- What are the problems/advantages of editing a journal/book that is defined by gender (i.e. all women's writing)?
- In what ways do you see women's writing surfacing in academic publications which have traditionally been vehicles for men's writing?
- How have issues in current feminist theory influenced your editorial practice?
- How do you think women fit into the exchange economy of editorial practice? Is editing an issue of economy or an issue of aesthetics, or both?

If these questions seem too slanted, feel free to ignore any or all of them in discussing your role as an editor. We are most interested in presenting a collection of differing viewpoints on the subject of editing which illustrates the diversity and ever-expanding participation by women. We are trying to solicit work from women who have edited publications which might be considered "separatist," and from those for whom gender is not a conspicuous part of their editorial agenda.

Please limit your response to 1-10 pages. Also include a separate, brief paragraph describing the factual data on your publication (when the publication began, where it's available, how long you have been editor, format, etc.). Feel free to forward this letter to other women editors.

Thank you for your participation.

Sincerely,

Jena Osman   Juliana Spahr

Susan Bee

Editing *M/E/A/N/I/N/G* magazine, I have had the opportunity to publish writing by artists I admire and artists with whom I was not acquainted; I've gotten to know them and their work better. Editing the writing of other artists, art historians, critics, and poets has given me a chance to confront opinions other than my own and to open myself up to multiple viewpoints on issues such as racism, feminism, longevity in art, motherhood, as well as the aesthetic and ideological concerns of our contributors. This constant input of new ideas generated by the magazine has challenged me to push my artwork into new directions in both content and form.

Gender is crucial to *M/E/A/N/I/N/G*'s editorial practice. Mira Schor and I, as women artists and editors, have sought out and encouraged other women to be contributors. *M/E/A/N/I/N/G* has frequently addressed feminist art issues. However, unlike *Heresies*, *Women Artists News*, and other feminist art magazines, we have also directed ourselves to men and have published the writings of male writers. We are not interested in confining our audience to women only and want to broaden the spectrum of topics covered beyond the range of other feminist art publications. I think we've been able to cross over without losing our feminist focus or our male readership.

M/E/A/N/I/N/G has had some impact on the art world. We've published writers' first pieces and they've gone on to write for other publications. We've also gotten people to focus on topics and questions that we've raised, many of which are otherwise not addressed in the art world. However, it's hard for me to gauge the impact of the publication on the art world as a whole. For a small, independent publication our circulation is remarkably good—but, of course, it's much less than the glossy, ad-based art monthlies.

One of the hardest things for me as an editor is having to reject submissions. Having had many bad experiences of my own with rejections—I hate to do it to others. Sometimes we've asked for rewrites of poor articles and have been pleasantly surprised at the revisions. I like working with writers to improve their copy and to help them to lucidly put forward their ideas. Even if I don't agree with it, I am pleased when I can edit a piece and help the writer to express her or his point of view. Since many of our writers are visual artists who are not used to putting their ideas into words, editing *M/E/A/N/I/N/G* has often been challenging.

We have published many articles that discuss feminist theory and its relation to contemporary art practice. Our initial hope was to make the journal a place where practicing artists and theoretical issues could meet without killing each other off. I think we've succeeded in doing that. In the meantime, we have gone on to address specific topics. One of our liveliest forums was on motherhood and art. Thirty-one women artists wrote in answer to a series of questions by the editors. The answers, from women artists of different generations, ranged from personal to theoretical. Some women were grandmothers and some had infants: the differences and similarities in certain problems over time made for interesting reading.

One issue I would like to raise is the problem of power sharing and critical balance in the roles of co-editors. With two people involved in all the decision-making and the work, imbalances in functions and roles and various trade-offs naturally arise. It seems impossible to share equitably responsibilities as well as to share whatever benefits come from editing a magazine. These imbalances need to be discussed by the editors and the relationship between the editors has to be an open one where each party feels able to confront the other about the "underlying" issues. I believe that having a dual editorship is a strength as it permits a wider range of contacts and interests to be reached than often would be possible by a single editor.

Editing a nonprofit journal will always be a labor of love, no matter how many small grants one may get. So while I enjoy editing *M/E/A/N/I/N/G* — I have also gotten to regret the time it takes away from my other activities. At this point, we're in our eighth year, and we're busy editing *M/E/A/N/I/N/G* #15, which includes a forum on creativity and community, for Spring 1994.

M/E/A/N/I/N/G, a journal of contemporary art issues, was started in 1986. To date we have published 14 issues. We come out twice a year in May and November and have never been late. Susan Bee and Mira Schor are co-editors and publishers. Susan Bee designed all the issues. The format is 8 1/2 x 11, perfect bound, and has changed very little since the inception. Generally we run 56 pages of text without any pictures. Our lack of illustrations and advertising makes us unique among art publications.

Dodie Bellamy/Andrea Juno

Talking on Minna Street

Dodie Bellamy: Kathe Burkhart was here at New Langton Arts with the Abortion Project, and she said several New York artists didn't want to be in it—afraid to be part of an all-women's show, afraid to be thus marginalized, trivialized. Things have changed since then, I know, but did you have any problem with that when you did the *RE/Search* book on *Angry Women*?

Andrea Juno: I see both sides. I see that you have to develop a space where you're not competing, to establish one's identity, especially in the early forms of any politics; but the game then is to throw it out, so as not to get encrusted within identity.

Bellamy: I understand that at the recent Buffalo "New Coast" Writers' Conference, one of the panels addressed the issue of why so many writing magazines are so male dominated, and the answer came back, sheepish and lame, that women don't submit their work. Kevin and I started *Mirage #4/Period[ical]* about a year and a half ago, without fanfare, and almost immediately we started getting submissions from men. On a bet we withheld announcing our new venture from one local male writer, known for his aggression in getting his work out, to see how long it would take him. It was a hoax, or joke. Within thirty days not only did we get his submission but also a stamped return envelope—and he lives six blocks away. Are men more "professional"? I don't know. And ours is a very slight zine, it's not big or glamorous. I don't think it's that women want to succeed less than men: perhaps it goes back to what Kathleen Fraser said about women's writing—that women tend to be more tentative. Submission in this sense is, oddly, a kind of aggression, and only recently has it become okay for women to be sexually aggressive—in matters of publication it's the same. And I'm the same way. Only rarely have I sent my work out unsolicited, and when I do it tends to get rejected.

Juno: I was lucky when I did *Angry Women*, for the women's movement had been in full swing (*although, of course, it had been moved totally, totally backwards*). Because I didn't want to do a book of "just women," and I didn't even want to deal with quote-unquote women's issues; I kind of sidestepped the whole issue and asked myself only, "What is happening that's really creative?" and, at that moment, in the arts, I thought—it was all women! I couldn't help that! It was women who were the locus of the most intense and revelatory issues of our times, issues of gender, issues of power, issues of the economy of the last 2,500 years. (I can't think of many heterosexual male artists who are really hitting on the sensitive issues of our times.)

Bellamy: It's a bit disingenuous to say, "Oh, it's just a coincidence that they're all women, that these were the most artistic people of 1989" or whenever. The very title points out that they're women—you don't call it *Neat Artists or Angry People*.

Juno: I had a lot of problems with this—I still do. Three or four of the women showed immediate anger about the title, although oddly enough, not because of the "women" but because of the "angry." One woman burst out, "I'm not angry!" although her entire performance art is like this *total shriek of anger*. Now, yes it's true, that she's not angry on a day-to-day level. But I thought, "Whoa! Why does this word carry so much weight, and why do these women want to distance themselves so far from this word?" Once I had received a similar response from three other women, as though anger was un-cool, or un-sexy, I started thinking of the "Angry Young Men" of the fifties and sixties—the amorphous James Dean types whose anger *was* sexy, because anger is one of the sanctioned responses that men have, and women don't. No man would protest being featured in a book called *Angry Young Men*, do you think?

Bellamy: Coming from a lower class background, anger was one of the few options open to women. I couldn't act sensitive, I was called a "big baby." Yet as I operate here, in a middle-class world, if you're angry, it makes you look like you haven't arrived. If you're at the top, what's there to feel angry about? In pop culture, there's a sexy angry woman, who pouts down runways and sulks through George Michael's videos, and sulks through jeans commercials.

Juno: But isn't that an anger that's attached to powerlessness? The Anna Magnani type, boiling with rage. The figure you describe—she's not Ms. 45. I think she's a modern version of the hysterical woman, who's been around with us for ages. The women in *Angry Women* in fact are very functioning, civilized, healthy, expressional, not given to excesses of rage—with a few exceptions we could both name.

Bellamy: And confident and glamorous—I noticed how many of the women were photographed nude (at least the white women). You have to have a certain confidence before you strip down for the readers of *RE/Search*.

Juno: [*Laughs*] I call it "sex positive." It's important that we counter the Catherine Mackinnon definition of what a feminist should be, and that we own our own sexuality enough to reinvent it from our own rules. This generation is one of the first to be able to play with sexuality in a way that our mothers and grandmothers couldn't, though their struggles and sacrifices remain important to me and very moving.

Bellamy: I'm often envious of women in the visual arts, who seem to have more permission and a larger vocabulary with which to deal with issues of sexuality than we writers have, even in this day. Not long ago I was telling Lyn Hejinian that I went to an Open Studio tour, a group show of a women's art class. It was the most vapid, bathetic romanticism, endless watercolors of nude women. As I looked, I was stunned to realize that in painting, in any of the visual arts, you can show pubic hair all over the place, and it's nothing more than a sentimentalized cliché of bad art, but if you use the words "pubic hair" within a written text, it's still aggressive, even shocking to some. Lyn replied that we writers then have the advantage, because who would want to say "pubic hair" if it meant the same as "bicycle"? It brings up funny questions of representation and of, as you say, freedom itself.

Juno: But now this freedom is rapidly disappearing again. Now these books are coming out, saying, "Yes, we're feminists, but we don't really like the political stuff." As if women have actually even *won* any freedoms, as if there *were* day care, as if abortion weren't almost *illegal*, as if women *had* achieved economic parity with men! It's shocking, really: Susan Faludi's *Backlash* just came out—you'd think there'd be a little bit of time before another actual backlash, but no.

Bellamy: "How do you think women fit into the exchange economy of editorial practice? Is editing an issue of economy or an issue of aesthetics, or both?" I think of this young woman who I work with, a poet applying to graduate school in creative writing, and I invited her to submit her work to *Mirage #4/Period[ical]* and she said that she didn't feel that she was developed enough as a poet, that she didn't deserve publication, that she wanted to wait at least two years until she had some *graduate school* under her belt. Internalized censorship does quite as much damage as any external form of censorship.

Juno: In our country, let's face it, we're not given keys to analysis—we're given keys to fashion. We're sound-bite oriented. What's important is to develop political theory and to put it into practice, to explain the inexplicable. To investigate the borderland areas, the slashes between the polarities—

Bellamy: The "slashes"?

Juno: Good slash Evil, Male slash Female, Either slash Or—to try to get into that slash and hopefully circumnavigate the way that most political oppositional thinking usually ends up becoming the very enemy it opposes. The perfect example is the "feminist" thought of Catherine Mackinnon and Andrea Dworkin, who are becoming the oppositional character they think they're against. The male power structure has, from time immemorial, proscribed that women can't enjoy sex, that sexuality is out of our domain, and here they are unconsciously aping this structure and dictating to other women what women's sexuality should be . . . I don't make any bones about it—I'm not some hypocritical "objective" journalist. I don't know how to write, but I know how to talk, and I love to have conversations with people that can illuminate ideas I want to illuminate. Obviously I'm going to pick people who can teach me things also. Avital Ronell, my God, is so massively brilliant I can always learn something amazing from her. I would never, ever put in people who I don't like what they're saying, and, if people say something I don't like, that I disagree with, I cut it out! In *Pranks*, for example, Boyd Rice talked about his drug use, and these terrible pranks with dogs—we took all that out and basically made it all up. And that was of course, before his horrible involvement with the White Aryan Resistance.

Bellamy: Would you have done a book like *Bob Flanagan: Super-Masochist,* if Bob had been a woman?

Juno: I'm not really interested in women being masochists

because . . . I see it too much. And I react against it viscerally. Turn on the TV, watch any movie, go down to the street corner, listen to your neighbors, you'll see women as unconscious masochists, re-enacting traumas from the past. What I found most illuminating about Bob was his illness, the fact of his facing death, and how his sexuality came into power, his real, conscious connections between his early childhood, his illness, his art, and his libido. How many people can make that kind of clear connection? In all my books I try to counter society's notion of the artist as marginalized, scary, dangerous, unkempt, sadistic weirdo with the fact of someone like Bob, sweet, pleasant, courteous, yet with a set of free-floating, radical ideas. Culture keeps a control system over those who have a deeper tap into the creative unconscious, and I love to play off culture's expectations.

Bellamy: I've been lucky and had the support early on of several female editors. When I was writing poetry, Julia Penelope Stanley had me read at this lesbian reading at an MLA Convention—there I was, in front of hundreds of people, reading with Marilyn Hacker and Elsa Gidlow. I was totally starstruck. The second piece of prose writing I ever did was "The Debbies I Have Known." Bruce Boone suggested I send it to the writer Rachel Blau DuPlessis, of whom I'd never heard at the time. And she accepted it for *Feminist Studies.* A whole realm of possibility, of validation, opened before me. At that point, I remember—this was the early 80's—I was studying with Kathleen Fraser at S.F. State, and Carolyn Burke came to speak to our class about the new French feminisms of Julia Kristeva, Luce Irigaray, Helene Cixous. It was a class so exciting that afterwards the women in the bathroom talked about it like we were on drugs. Anyway Burke said that being published in *Feminist Studies* had changed her entire life. Imagine how I felt! Actually it *didn't* change my life, but—[*Laughs.*]. And then, years later, when Carla Harryman asked me to contribute to a special section of *Poetics Journal* she was editing, I felt a different gratification, that of being taken seriously, perhaps for the first time, as an intellectual. —How do you work with a male colleague [V. Vale]? Is there a gender struggle between you?

Juno: We're usually pretty much in synch: there's nothing he would object to if I wanted to do it. *Angry Women* was my idea, whereas *Incredibly Strange Music* is more his thing. Vale does all the transcribing of these tapes, not only a laborious chore, but one filled with creativity. It's not a straight transcription, it's highly edited. It's an art form wherein the spoken word gets transcribed into its very different cousin, the written word. It would be unconscionable to present an interview as given—*remember that, Kevin*! Oral communication is a dream-like transmission, that stops and starts, that describes a story, that starts a theme, that gets picked up three days later. Everyone gets a copy of the interview—we want their further participation, although only a few bizarre male egos actually ask us to change history and to re-write what they said. The fact of the matter is that we present everyone in such a positive light that it would have to be a personal quirk. We don't write intros that say, "Now you're going to hear from a pathetic shit." If they're in *RE/Search*, it's because we revere them, we polish them up like diamonds, to a bright light. Our editing process makes everyone sound intelligent, even myself. We do this because most media, faced with alternate ideas, especially if encased in alternative people, turns them into freaks so that they can be dismissed easily. How much better for the ideas—which are, by and large, eloquently presented anyhow, believe me, we're not inventing interesting people out of total nutcases—to be given this polish of presentation.

Bellamy: Aren't you then valorizing these people, turning them into culture heroes, especially if you're editing out anything negative about them?

Juno: This is a real thorny problem, a minefield for me personally. On one level, yes, that was the original project, to present slices of a person, because, obviously who are you gonna kid? This is a book where someone will be given at most twenty pages, and even if I had twenty hours of videotape, I couldn't make an objectified life, I couldn't capture a person's thought. You either expose your agenda or you don't. You either present a person's personality mask, which is totally high school popularity contest, or you deny their multi-faceted nature. Like myself. I usually have my mask on, I'm trained, talkative bright, cheerful, where actually I'm a very shy, fearsome soul. Not "actually," because my mask is now part of me, and a big one. So Vale and I originally wanted to present ideas we were interested in that would reframe issues, whatever the successes and failures of that are, and only incidentally to re-make role models. The minefield, after thirteen years, is watching people who we have "valorized"—people are not static, fixed objects, and that sometimes they grow and sometimes they [*laughs*] devolve. I wish I had control over some of these people, but I don't!

Bellamy: I've always had a hard time accepting any kind of authorial position, or authority. I remember Kathleen always used to talk about women writers being on the margins, in this liminal space, but that isn't *abject* enough for me, I always think of myself as *outside* the margin. You too?

Juno: Before we did *Modern Primitives*, you have to remember, only a handful of people, outside of the gay community, in only a few cities, were into piercing and tattooing. Maybe some biker people. It wasn't the phenomenon it is now. In fact when we did that book we were scared to death we were going to lose our entire *RE/Search* readership, everybody would hate us, it wouldn't sell. Little did we know there'd be piercing parlors, piercing on the street. It was a very different climate. Linda Evangelista's navel wasn't pierced yet. But one of the men featured in *Modern Primitives* has gone on to great fame, has started workshops and developed a whole metaphysics of piercing, which is totally bogus, saying that if you get pierced your consciousness will change for the better: well, it won't. Okay, we did valorize him, and now we're seeing the consequences of that. But I don't know what to do. Because I do love the art of the interview, yet I'm fettered by the idea that the people in the books will "become" their own profiles, which is appalling. I don't know what's going to happen. You walk on a razor sharp edge. You don't want the baby—the ideas—thrown out with the bathwater—the dismissal of the thinker. If you present the idea, through Vale's transparent editing, with a certain nobility, are you then valorizing the person? Look at the anti-Communist films of the 50's, where Communists are invariably sweaty beady-eyed creeps. Women are constantly vilified when we step out of our place. I don't want to have to defend *Madonna*, but look at what the press has done to her. First, she "slept her way to the the top." Then, she's "ambitious." Now, she's "over." This is the narrative of the status quo, that women shouldn't be sensual, shouldn't disturb gender relationships, and shouldn't want power. She's constantly being smashed, and yet look at someone like—I don't know—*[laughs]* Michael Bolton!

This conversation was begun on Sunday, November 28, 1993, and transcribed and edited by Kevin Killian on December 10-27, 1993—"*I'm not into an exclusionary politics*"—Andrea Juno.

Lee Ann Brown

From CUZ to zuk

This semi-palindromic title refers to two publications from very different milieus that were among many that inspired me to edit and publish.

"CUZ" was edited by Richard Meyers when he was the coordinator for the Monday night readings at the Poetry Project. It was my first NYC publication, soon after I made my NYC "debut" in his reading series in Spring, 1988. Alphabetically, I was listed before William Burroughs on the back cover of issue #2 with Maggie Dubris, Susie Timmons, Dennis Cooper, Eileen Myles, Will Patton and others. I was inspired by Richard's aesthetic sense and how he and Mike DeCapite worked, diligently retyping the "French spacing" after file conversions, going to a bindery and doing it themselves to save money, getting friends to help collate, and arranging the poets' banquet he threw complete with absinthe, wild game, Deborah Harry, and a lost exquisite corpse. The magazine was kinda funky and elegant at the same time.

"zuk," named for Louis Zukofsky, was one of the most beautiful little mags I had ever seen, edited by Claude Royet-Journoud, published by Editions Spectres Familiers in Paris. It arrived in the mail while I was working at the Poetry Project. It was in a small format (4 x 6), letter pressed black and red on a few sheets of creamy paper. It held language/lyric French translations of American poets such as Norma Cole, Ted Pearson, Rosmarie Waldrop, Larry Eigner, Kit Robinson, Michael Palmer, Charles Bernstein and new work from the French: Jean Daive, Jacques Roubaud, Françoise de Laroque, Dominique Fourcade, Emmanuel Hocquard, Joseph Guglielmi and others.

Other main inspirations include United Artists, Burning Deck, Angel Hair. . . . I remember Anne Waldman saying to me one summer ('87) in Boulder, "why don't you start a magazine?" I thought about it for a few moments and decided books were more permanent and needed doing. I later found that Bernadette Mayer's *Sonnets* manuscript had been sitting in a drawer for a while and that one publisher had fallen through. Besides, who was going to publish me? I might as well do it myself. But I shouldn't do myself first, I reasoned. I should create a context. Anne also emphasized how many great poets would not be in print if it wasn't for their friends' efforts. So I set out to do some inspirers right.

Tender Buttons

Tender Buttons #1: *Sonnets* by Bernadette Mayer, 1989.
Tender Buttons #2: *Not a Male Pseudonym* by Anne Waldman, 1990.
Tender Buttons #3: *Trimmings* by Harryette Mullen, 1991.
Tender Buttons #4: *Agnes Lee* by Agnes Lee Dunlop Wiley, 1992.
Tender Buttons #5: *Lawn of Excluded Middle* by Rosmarie Waldrop, 1993.
Tender Buttons #6: *Silent Teachers Remembered Sequel* by Hannah Weiner, 1994.
Pamphlet: *Cultivate* by Lee Ann Brown, Summer 1991.
Tender Broadsides #1: Spring 1993.
> Poems by Lee Ann Brown, Liz Fodaski, Ted Pearson, Laynie Brown, Lisa Jarnot, Judith Goldman, Jennifer Moxley, Sianne Ngai, Danine Ricerito and James Thomas Stevens.

Of course, the name is a tribute to Stein's great poem, *Tender Buttons*. I think of the books as multi-faceted objects, written from many angles, and unfolding in different ways, like Stein's "cubist" writings.

Parts of Bernadette Mayer's *Sonnets* were later reprinted by New Directions in *The Bernadette Mayer Reader*. It took me forever just to type them all into the Mac and I was constantly grilling everyone I knew who published about how to lay it out. I had no idea! I based the size and design on Bernadette's design of Ted Berrigan's *Sonnets*.

For the cover I made a stat of a drawing by her daughter, Marie and asked Thomson Shore to print it in blue with a black background. We matched the blue to Bernadette's favorite in her Ukrainian scarf—that blue in late evening when the sky is about to turn to black. Since the publication, Bernadette has written more sonnets.

Anne Waldman's *Not a Male Pseudonym*, which is a love poem she wrote to Bernadette in the 70's, had been hidden in a trunk since Anne read it at the Poetry Project and incensed her mother. I tried to save money by printing the text myself, which I did with the aid of Frank Murphy on the Poetry Calendar's offset press in Brooklyn. The cover, a painting by

Donna Dennis, was printed by Mercury of Magic Circle Press off Union Square.

Roberto Bedoya, then the literary programmer of Intersection in San Francisco, had heard Harryette Mullen read *Trimmings* and he thought I would like the work. A while later I met her at the Ear Inn when she came to the East Coast to teach at Cornell. Directly inspired by Gertrude Stein's *Tender Buttons*, *Trimmings* deftly and nondogmatically plays with how women's clothing forms perceptions of gender, race and body image. Loughran O'Connor did the cover art and design, and it was reviewed in the *Village Voice* by Eileen Myles among other places.

Agnes Lee by Agnes Lee Dunlop Wiley is a memoir by my grandmother, published for her 90th birthday. The genesis of the book is an "I Remember"-esque list poem of "Things I'd Like To Do Again" which she began in 1927. It is composed in short episodic sections.

Lawn of Excluded Middle by Rosmarie Waldrop, is a continuation of the project she began in *The Reproduction of Profiles*, which was published by New Directions. It works to refigure sentences from Wittgenstein and investigate questions of the feminine and its relation to the space of logic and the brave new physics.

Silent Teachers Remembered Sequel by Hannah Weiner was just published this fall and is in two sections. Both are dictated by voices Hannah beams in, filtered through her interests in theory, performance and politics. The first is her manifesto of who is "teaching" us as poets as referred to in the intermediate section: "we must integrate into the next generation:" "the next generation could be the one that is done and gone and who is teaching you now." It has the characteristic Hannahesque immediacy of being very present in the act of writing: in the middle of the first piece there is a page with a scribble which reads: "drawing interlude scratch." "Silent teachers" ends as she is writing until the paper runs out: "next please omit strategic ending fallover anymore// paper left hum." The only sound left: humming of the typewriter. No more words for now. The second section, "Remembered Sequel," was written earlier, also dictated, and is in a paragraph form, reminiscent, I think, of Stein's *How to Write*. Hannah even "heard" half of the blurbs on the back, from the likes of W.C. Fields, Barrett Watten and noa Kleinman, an "old anarchist" who dictated the poem, "the comm a capitol ma." This rhymes nicely with Bernadette's blurbs by Hawthorne, Stein and others on the back of her self-published *Utopia*. How's that for refiguring subjectivity? Brian Schorn did the cover using elements of a high school photograph of Hannah in Providence with a "Classical" High pennant in the background.

Blurbs were fun to get. I got in contact with poets I always wanted to talk with, like Ron Silliman, John Ashbery, Gwendolyn Brooks . . . since you're being an advocate for someone else's work that you both have an interest in, it's easy.

More on the gender issue: I remember talking to a poet whom I greatly admire but who made me feel kind of tongue-tied when I was first in NYC. He asked me about Tender Buttons and the concept behind it. I tried to explain the link in my mind between Luce Irigaray's concept of multiplicity, in "The Sex Which Is Not One," Joe Brainard's beautiful logo: (double pansies clothed in dress and coat), and the vulva of which she writes so wonderfully. Tender Buttons are "the two lips," nipples, clits, skin, multiplicitous sites of pleasure, both physical and conceptual.

"A woman touches herself constantly without anyone being able to forbid her to do so, for her sex is composed of two lips which embrace continually. Thus, within herself she is already two—but not divisible into ones—who stimulate each other."

He asked if and why I would publish only women. I said I didn't know yet, and that it wasn't absolute. I later realized I had been talking to an editor of the otherwise wonderful *Anthology of New York Poets* that had included Bernadette at 25 as the only woman in it. What was that all about? What about Barbara Guest? Alice Notley? Who else? (And the *New American Poetry, 1945-1960*. Only Helen Adam and Denise Levertov. And racially how fucked up.)

On at least two occasions, both by male independent publishers who had done no more than one woman's book in their whole historic run, it was said of me: "O, she's the one who does *women's* books." First I was insulted that I would be characterized that way—one of the main reasons I am doing only women's books is because you guys did only men—it's necessary! But then later I thought, well maybe they were complimenting me.

It's complicated, because there are contemporary male poets who need books published, who are neglected, and who I love dearly for inspiring me too. To quote the Breeders, "I just want to get along." But as long as presses who publish only or mostly men are thought of as "normal" and called "presses," and presses who happen to publish only women are labeled "that one who does women's books," we have a problem. This is where the economic issue comes into play also—since I'm strapped for funds I need to be clear about my priorities. Tender Buttons and Kelsey St. Press, are the only presses that I know of that publish mainly experimental poetry by women. I publish work by men in broadsides, pamphlets or in magazine issues I edit (*West Coast Line, Crow,* . . .), schedule men in poetry reading series, and teach work by men in my classes, but since books are such a primary commodity in this culture, I choose to invest my time, energy and money for women.

As I pointed out in the small press panel in Buffalo last spring, I didn't make a conscious decision to only publish women when I began—I just formulated the concept of the press out of what I felt to be most exciting at the time in my life and work. And when I interrogated the idea further I felt at ease with the decision. I thought people would naturally understand the necessity and meaning of the project, but trying to explain it does help to further articulate it.

Even though headway has been made in realizing the need for recognition of literature by "Others," the work that gets support tends to bear overt markers of such an identity, or serves as a confessional log of wrongs inflicted upon the author as a member of this oppressed group. Is this what we mean by politically correct? Espousing only preapproved controversies in a manner to be understood like a TV commercial or press release? Tender Buttons is dedicated to publishing poetry that poses questions of gender, race, and material reality but it's essential that this be done in a formally innovative way. Change the language to change the world. We need the freedom to challenge ourselves as writers, to be as difficult as we want to be without apology.

Women Poet Editors & Publishers in Providence

Providence has the fortune of being a magnet for poets, one of the few cities of this size to house such a gathering, resulting in the fortunate convergence of several literary publications edited by unique and extraordinary women with various yet related concerns. The Brown Graduate Writing Program serves as a sort of institutional vortex next to and around a truly diverse poetic community with sensitive tendrils out to both coasts. And we have great role models in Rosmarie Waldrop of Burning Deck and C.D.Wright of Lost Roads.

Tender Buttons
Lee Ann Brown
54 East Manning Street #3
Providence, RI 02906

The Impercipient
editor: Jennifer Moxley
61 East Manning Street
Providence, RI 02906-4008
8 1/2 x 11, stapled.
In its 4th issue, begun in February, 1992. "The Silent Pillow of a Generation." Dedicated to the lyric, and what younger, not so or unpublished writers are doing with it. Please see her piece in this issue for more insight into her strategies.

Black Bread
c/o Sianne Ngai
46 Preston Street
Providence, RI 02906
Edited by Jessica Lowenthal & Sianne Ngai. Varying formats, perfect bound. Available through Small Press Distribution.
  This magazine publishes mainly, though not exclusively, women. There is a strong Providence, New York, and San Francisco presence. Begun in 1992 and now in its fourth issue, a special issue of collaborations is just out (à la *Locus Solus*).

Torque
c/o Liz Fodaski
PO Box 118 Canal St. Station
New York, NY 10013
Format: 8 1/2 x 11, stapled. Started by Liz Fodaski after she left Providence and moved back to NYC. In its first issue, January, 1994. The strong torquing between words and that network of poetry flashing between NYC and Providence. First issue is free. Bi-annual. Submissions, correspondence welcome, second issue in Fall 1994. I conducted a phone interview with Ms. Fodaski during her receptionist job for an ad agency on Lafayette Street where she was able to Xerox the first issue for free. We are constantly interrupted by chic muzak as she answers other lines.

How has editing influenced your other work?
I'm less self-absorbed about my poetry, less individually focused—more spread out, more influences. I'm being more interested in multiplicitous forms, rather than hyper-driven by an individual sense of product.

[Monkees: "I'm a Believer"]

Does gender play a role in your editorial process?
The 2nd issue will highlight inspirational women writers who've influenced my generation of writers. It will be a combination of homage & admiration & inspiration. I want to highlight those women who've been inspirational in their innovation & their great works.

Power or subversion of it?
That has everything to do with the initial impulse of *Torque*, the power of putting work out and the subversion of the powers of exclusion, publishing people who've never been published before.

Obligations?
I guess the obligation to allow poetry to be distributed and read in formats, venues, areas where interested parties have access to it and it will be seen and heard.

What are the problems/advantages of editing a journal/book that is defined by gender?
That's not my agenda. I hate the argument that publishing only women is exclusive. I didn't want any limitations. I can allow myself to highlight certain things and not be exclusive.

[Tossin' & Turnin']

I also did an interview with a secret informant from Battle Creek, MI, the anonymous editor of Frontier Press.

How's it going?
Pretty ghostly so far. I'm doing a continuation of Harvey Brown's Frontier Press (H.D.'s *Hermetic Definitions*, William Carlos Williams' *Spring & All*, *Gunslinger* by Ed Dorn, Ed Sanders' *Peace Eye,* and other bootlegs.)

Format?
Broadsides & chapbooks. Duncan bootlegs and other out of print &/or unpublished materials of contemporary American poetry.

How will people get it?
It will get to them. Don't call us we'll call you.

Does gender play a role in your editorial practice?
No, not really. Marginalization in general does. Experimental disappeared poetry. "New hope for the disappeared," you know, the disappearing manuscript. . . . Subversion of power subversion of um the art pigs who hoard manuscripts & corpses. Yeah, it's like same story, new decade (like Norman Holmes Pearson).

Don't you feel you are exerting power in publishing anonymously?
I feel like it throws more stuff out into the community, it opens up the information lines to stuff that would otherwise never be seen.

What obligations do you answer to as an editor?
On a basic technical level, to present the information in the form intended by the author.

Anything else?
I want to say that Frontier Press publications have been distributed throughout the US & Canada.

Cydney Chadwick

Dear Jena and Juliana:

I think editing's influenced my work by perhaps making me more cautious about my writing appearing in print. It's my impression that an editor's work comes under greater scrutiny by those readers who are aware that you're an editor. I'm still undecided if this puts one in a position of power (power as impetus), or if this type of examination doesn't cause a tendency toward self-subversion. But on a less personal level, and interpreting what you're asking us to address (editing as power or subversion of power), every time a new, uninitiated reader picks up *Avec*, is intrigued by the work and subscribes—that's power, power to influence, power to expand audience for the kind of writing I publish. There's a lot of cynicism in small press about its capability to attract a varied and expanding readership, but judging from the correspondence I receive, *Avec* is being read and subscribed to by people who've come across it in bookstores, at bookfairs, or have heard of it by word of mouth. On the other hand, every time *Avec* gets a grant, or attracts a new reader, I see it as being subversive to an established set of aesthetics (and literary power structure).

When I founded *Avec*, I wasn't personally acquainted with any of the writers I wanted to publish (save one); I knew only their work. This enabled me to answer only to myself when I went to edit (as an "outsider," I didn't feel indebted or compelled to publish any particular writer, or group of writers).

In January 1990, *Avec* was granted non-profit status; this means that over time I've endeavored to build up a constituency (not just casual readers) through a membership program. The ideology behind traditional non-profits is that you're there to serve your constituency, so I spend a lot of time thinking about what I want to do with the journal on a personal level, versus *Avec*'s constituency. For example, many requested that I also publish critical work and reviews in *Avec*. But I wanted to reserve the pages for poetry and prose, so I decided to publish a companion volume of essays, reviews, and poetics—*Witz* (edited by Christopher Reiner).

Taking the non-profit approach and keeping a constituency in mind, has, I think, led me to take more risks than I would have if *Avec* hadn't gone non-profit, had remained merely a hobby. I probably wouldn't have started the book press, because

I could have done an occasional book and called it an issue of the journal, or an anthology of prose and called it an issue of the journal, and so on.

I'm curious to see how taking this tack will have served me (and *Avec*) in retrospect. Since the approach deviates from the way a lot of small presses are run, I feel like I'm experimenting, and this keeps the experience of publishing from being repetitious, a grind.

In response to your other question about women's writing in academic publications, I see an increase in books and articles published by women, but the majority of these are women writing about women's work for primarily a female audience, leading me to believe that women as writers and thinkers continue to be (here it comes, the "m" word).

Naturally feminist theory can't help but have an effect on the way I read and think, but I don't consciously call it up when reviewing work for the journal. However, as a friend and I have discussed, the male-dominated canon has had such an insidious effect on one's reading; feminist theory assists me to remain cognizant of these effects, and call them into question when I read and edit the journal.

From both an editorial and reader's point of view, I'd say that within the last couple of years, and at the present moment, women are writing such interesting, provocative work. I've speculated as to why, why now? Is it that more books by women are being published, meaning I have more access (at one time) to current work? Could it be that many male writers are still preoccupied with, as a woman I know calls it, "staking the flag," in poetic territories, leaving women "free" to do their own work? (I continue to see an absence of women's work being brought under discussion (much) in these so-called territories). Or is it, do you suppose, as another friend has speculated, women have more permission with their writing these days, they're paying more attention to each other's work, and supporting each other to a greater extent?

Perhaps, though, you aren't of the same opinion? Regardless, I'm interested to know what you and the other participants think about this, and hope the topic can be touched on in future discussions.

All the best,
Cydney

Avec journal was founded in 1988. It is distributed by Inland Book Company, Bookpeople, and Small Press Distribution. Avec books was founded in 1992.

Maxine Chernoff

A Home in the Mind

Since 1986, I have co-edited *New American Writing*. Paul Hoover and I publish the magazine twice a year in an edition of 4000 copies. It uses glossy covers by local and national artists, usually printed in 4-colors, and runs from 150-200 pages/issue. Though it is primarily a poetry journal, it frequently includes essays, interviews, stories, and reviews. The magazine has many library and personal subscribers but is unusual in that it is distributed primarily through bookstore and newsstand sales, which account for approximately 3200 copies per issue: 2200 with Ingram and a variety of other distributors.

New American Writing publishes the most interesting and important writing we receive. Approximately half of our issue is solicited. Approximately one-third of each issue contains writers we've never published before, though we tend to publish certain writers repeatedly. The women among them are Marjorie Welish, Ann Lauterbach, Lydia Davis, Rosmarie Waldrop, Barbara Guest, Hilda Morley, Elaine Equi, Susan Wheeler, Alice Notley, Anne Waldman, Carla Harryman, Carolyn Knox, Elizabeth Robinson, Connie Deanovich, and Wanda Coleman, for example. These women represent a wide variety of "experimental strategies."

Edited by a husband/wife team, *New American Writing* has no stated feminist agenda. The intelligent and innovative use of language doesn't appear to be gender-specific. However, the magazine does receive a high number of serious submissions by women, perhaps because it is a "general" magazine co-edited by a woman and has historically published a large number of women. Do women respond to my name on the masthead? Perhaps. Though I would like to think, as Paul Hoover has observed in his workshop at Columbia College, Chicago, that many of the best poets today simply are women. Their numbers may be disproportionately high in the general population.

As a writer and editor, I am skeptical of popular theories that ascribe different tendencies of mind to men and women. Surely, no one would be comfortable with the Aristotelian "Female is female by virtue of a certain lack of qualities" or Aquinas's belief that "woman is an imperfect man." Yet, when women use the more contemporary Freudian ideas rehabilitated by

Lacan that women are oceanic and men linear, they fall prey to over-simplification. Important writing is practiced by men and women. Unimportant writing is practiced by men and women. There is no one duller than, say, Sharon Olds, who linguistically titillates in poems seen as provocative, by readers of *New Yorker* poetry and the dreadful writing establishment, the same establishment that ignores many writers of both genders who are aware of the deeper possibilities of a text, who take on unexpected subject matter, and who explore what it means to be a human being in the most complex ways. But many publishers appealing to a larger market want caricatures of what it means to be male or female, Asian- or African-American. Rather than expand what is acceptable for any person to think or experience, they want contrived registers of identity-thought. If our existence as editors matters, it does so by expanding what is thought acceptable. However, *New American Writing*, with its fine poets and high aesthetic considerations, is read by 4,000 whereas the *New Yorker*, with its Sharon Olds' caricatures of gender-appropriate thought, enjoys a circulation of 600,000.

A final observation: As a writer of rather strange but finally "domestic" fiction, I have recently enjoyed acceptance of my prose at major houses (Vintage and Simon and Schuster). When I published my novel, *Plain Grief*, however, a male editor, the same one who purchased Brad Easton Ellis's *American Psycho* in which women are skinned and murdered, claimed that I wasn't "being fair" to my male character. Still, writing on subjects that New York editors broadly accept as female, I am achieving acceptance of my fiction at that level. When Paul Hoover wrote a novel about being a conscientious objector during the Viet Nam War, it was also published by Vintage. Writing about the war, even taking an anti-war stance is acceptable male practice. However, his more recent novel is a character-driven and zanily domestic farce about a man content in the domestic realm. This novel is having far more difficulty finding a major publisher. Has he broken some unwritten rule about male writing in the domestic realm? A novel I recently reviewed for the *New York Times* convinces me of the answer. If a man writes about the domestic realm, he must present himself as too good for its constraining social constructs. His talents of mind and body are too large for the small world of women and children. Ironically, this is also a theme in much domestic fiction in which a woman frees herself of limiting domestic constraints. Treated by a man, however, this rebellion often takes on a misogynist cast.

Are there, then, accepted "subject matter" and limits to

accepted subject matter that large publishers endorse? Even as we approach the end of the century and millennium, a woman's place is still supposed to be "in the home" and a man's "in the world." But the mind is everyone's home, male and female alike. The writers of our time who will be important in retrospect give full reign to that most lively of dwelling places.

Susan Clark, Catriona Strang, Lisa Robertson

"I want someone to say what you say" "We can just keep publishing the work we want to read and there it is!" "I like its rant" "My back is killing me from carrying heavy books" that "I don't think about gender, I just publish what I like" stuff "We are not we" "and the wages fall" "Editing is noticeable"

"It's supposed to be an object lesson."

Susan Clark, Catriona Strang, and Lisa Robertson edit *Raddle Moon* and *Giantess*.

Dorothy Cosand, Danika Dinsmore, Angela Oaks

Dogma

"What is today?/Today is/the 8th/the 8th of September/ Wednesday night/Wednesday night/This is our interview /What time is it?/It is a quarter till no actually it's 20 till. Our clocks are always off/20 till 10/It's mighty late/20 till 11/Oh shit/It's late/I have to go to work in 12 hours/I know I know/yep/

"So first question why Hyena?/It was Angela's idea/Was it? 'Cause I wanted to draw one. No. & too because it is an ugly beast utterly despised/I like the idea of laughing hyena/I like the idea of fringe hyena, you know. They eat corpses & hang out on the edges of villages/Yeah/The saddest sight that I ever saw was at the Los Angeles Zoo, the hyena cage & there was a hyena all by himself or herself sitting in the corner all crunched up, looking out at everyone & it was so depressing. I've never been to a zoo since/Wow/'Cause hyenas aren't supposed to be like that/Nope/It's sad/& actually it was a tossup . . . the first magazine I called Irregular, I had Irregular on all the pages of stuff/Yeah that was the idea/& then Angela drew an image that was like—That's it!/How can you draw irregular?/It's called Hyena because I drew a hyena/It was originally Irregular I remember, because we thought it was gonna be irregular & come out irregularly/We *wanted* it to be erratic & irregular/Now our press is Irregular Press . . . Right so it was close, it was neck'n'neck/Tossup/

"Why are the contributors in the first two issues exclusively *women*? . . . Because we only asked women!/True we only solicited from women/We only solicited from women why? . . . I said that I felt it was empowering for women to have a magazine exclusively theirs . . . & at first we were saying men have been able to edit & be in any kind of magazine that they wanted to/Yeah, right, we also said that if men wanted to submit that they could under a woman's name since women had to do that for so long/Which would be interesting because I'd wonder if we could tell the difference/Right/It's like that DeKooning quote/Exactly/You thought it was a woman & we're like—No/Except for he said 'trousers' & women don't say trousers I mean I don't/That's true/But it still sounded like a woman's voice . . . We say 'pantaloons'/I would be very intrigued to see if we could tell/& then Danika you said that/That . . . women were more likely to submit things that they wouldn't normally submit to a magazine because they'd feel empowered to do so. We've gotten submissions from women we've never heard of, local writers who might not normally submit to a magazine . . . & would feel confident to submit to a magazine that they knew was all women/I actually think the whole seed idea grew out of that Naropa summer week of men/Yeah/You know, I'm not listening to another masturbation poem/ Another fucking goddamn/Another rape poem another murder poem/Robert Creeley poem/As long as I live/*Yeah I got the biggest fish in the river.*/*I have shit on my dick!* [cackling] . . . Like, damn! how many times, how many variations of this can I listen to?/I think that's when we really started goin', I've had it, I wanta hear what other women have to say/Yep but then I felt real uncomfortable with it . . . it felt like we got a lot of work this time where the person just gave us what we wanted to see/

"Well that leads into the next question what *are* we looking for? & I think when we say . . . It's primarily a woman's magazine I get a lot of responses like 'oh then I have to submit a feminist poem'/Exactly/& that's not what we want . . . What we want is to reach outta that to see other things that women are doing. When you have a typical, quote male magazine unquote the stuff that women get in is the feminist stuff/Yeah/You know the bitchy . . . & even though I was calling this the 'hag mag' I didn't necessarily want a hag rant or rave or anything like that/Yeah, I do think that the submissions that we've gotten have been colored by what people assume we wanta read, I mean obviously . . . & we actually are a lot more experimental & flexible than probably right now our submissions are gonna' show/Yeah/We don't want a *theme* magazine we don't want the mag poetry that deals with women's issues, we want to see how diverse women can be/Right right . . . the diversity of women's voices & authenticity of diversity of voices/That's why we're gonna have an issue on porn/Yep/What I'm afraid of is that it is gonna become another wimmin's world, you know white women writing about academic topics/How to make a wallhanging from toilet paper holders, you know—Fuck!/I think there's enough of that out there/We don't want any birthing poems/No poems about menstrual blood/Except for Bernadette's/Unless it's well written! . . . what it boils down to is somebody can send us something that we all think is horribly trite but if it's well written we go— Yeah/Period poems/If you just like tell the truth/Yeah! Yeah!

tell the truth!/Right, if you go out to fucking redneck bars &
two-step, fine! Don't be tryin' to act like tofu queen . . . know
your own self, be whatever you are. Be white trash . . . be/be
submissive/Yeah!/Don't write 'I am woman hear me
roar!'/Right/That's why I like your mom's stuff/yeah/'Cause
she's like I am a domesticated woman I am a beaten woman I
am/ Yeah yeah exactly/[chanting] 'I am black woman I am
white woman I am blue woman I am black & blue woman'
/The variety of your real experience is what counts/What's
amazing to me is that we can all come with our diverse back-
grounds & yet we will agree. We read everything out loud &
when we don't like it—BEEP!/The buzzer goes off, although
sometimes we'll skip to the ending & go, well maybe it gets
better/So that's what we look for/Honesty & integrity/Yes,
authenticity/All that trite stuff/Experiments!/I would like to
see a lot more experimental stuff . . . things that people don't
think they should send/Risktaking yeah/Pages-outta-their-
journal-bullshit!/Definitely/You know, I would rather see
spontaneity on a napkin/I want to see some porn/I was looking
through a portfolio & the woman had these paintings that had
taken her a long time & she had these doodles & I'm like oh
give me these doodles she's like that's just scribbles/The scribble
yeah!/That's why Bernadette Mayer's list was so awesome 'cause
it reads like you're talkin' to yourself/

   ". . . So . . . does anybody wanta say who they are? . . . What
they do?/Who are you?/ [singing] Whoooo are you, Hoo
Hoo Hoo Hoo, whoooo are you, Hoo Hoo Hoo Hoo/
We just three little girls like to sing/Three sexy hagamuffins/
Three songbirds/Nobody wants to say/Who are we? . . .
Well I'm graduating from Naropa this December with
an MFA in Writing & Poetics whatever that means/Means
you'll never get a job! Burger King!/Let's label one another!
/That's why I don't like saying I'm a feminist/Right/
Vegetarian/Right/Heterosexual/Talk about your work/What
you're interested in right now/Oh well I'm actually doing my
thesis on Bernadette which is really cool/Yeah/I love her
work/She's very fascinating/I'm doing a lot of experimenting . . . Like the 3:15 journals where we woke up, six of us
woke up at 3:15 in the morning & wrote/Why did you decide
3:15?/It just seemed like the middle of the night/Yep/& it was
just kinda an odd number that stuck/I think that Myshel & I
decided on 3:15 . . . & I've been working with dreams &
hypnogogic & hypnopompic states as well, kinda like what
Bernadette's doing/My understanding of the interview is like
what I do with the computer because I sit down & I take jour-

nal entries & letters & cut them up in the computer, mathematically decide, maybe throw the dice or something & then say ok I'm gonna' take every nine characters/Yeah you've always got this weird mathematical system when you do your cutups/I do/You & Jackson MacLow/Yeah/Yeah you know I've tried doin' it without that, randomly rip things up & then I can't deal with it, I sit there & count out . . . everything I do into nine, that's like my number [cackling]/Numba nine . . . I've been doing some of Lee Ann Brown's experiments too like oh shit what are those things called, where you take the letters of the name & you make a poem, I've been doing those . . . & also cutting up other people's work & taking out all the nouns verbs & adjectives of one poem & switching them to another poem/Which is actually what I do mathematically . . . I mean you can do it randomly but how do you know when you have something?/

"So Angela who are you/What do *you* do/I've been decorating the house/She's really a housewife/Yes/Hausfrau/I wanta see your painting that you're working on in the back, your masterpiece/Yeah, I can't decorate & paint at the same time but that's all I've been doing/She made a real cool table where'd it go?/It's in my study in the back I'm tired of it/Our furniture changes monthly/Painted a chair/Angela says she's not a writer/Well I haven't written in a year & a half, I've found some lovely plates. Found a plate with Ike & Mamie Eisenhower on it/She can make pins/Oh yes I made a pin with jesus on it. I have jesus jewelry that's what I do!/Oh look send for a free catalog/We're getting a jesus nitelite & I have a jesus necklace . . . I am acquiring things looking in flea markets for them/But she has a sharp editorial eye & ear/Yes/& nose/& cruel/She is mean/I'm mean I'm amused I feel good/When Angela says no Danika & I look at each other & go 'dare we say yes?'/I'm pretty nice/We're all nice/We're actually too nice for our own good I mean we obviously put this magazine out with our own fucking money/ Yeah!/Yes we've been prostituting ourselves/Right/For the money to put out this magazine/ That's right/Yeah so donations accepted gladly/Oh yes they are, send 'em in now/

"Is that it?/Yep"

We began *HyeNA* in the summer of 1992. The first issue made its appearance in April 1993 and the second issue came out in October 1993 (the third is due in April 1994). We originally planned four issues a year, but finances and time have limited us to two a year.

Dubravka Djuric

A Few Statements on Politics and Power in Culture

1. Co-editing *Mental Space*, a magazine for alternative arts in the late communist society of Yugoslavia in the eighties, meant co-editing an organ of a very special global approach to the arts. Discussions by artists, members of the Community for Space Investigation who were at the same time theoreticians, tended to speak about global approaches. Visual art was the central domain but the approach also included other interests as represented by this chart:

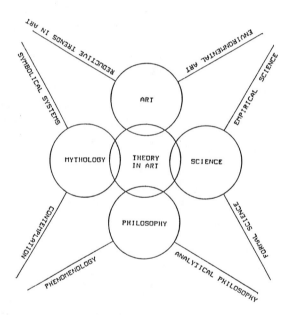

2. Editing, writing poetry, writing criticism, and translating are different modes of the same activity.

3. Poetical choices determine the politics and the economics of editing, writing, and translating. Poetical and political familiarity is presumed. Editorial and writing practice imply political

choice. Power in culture is in direct relation to power in politics. In a post-communist society as well as in a communist one, every aspect of a person's life, private and public equally, is marked with politics. (Similarly, periods of establishing communism and periods where it is in crisis, or of its end, are similar because of the same amount of chaos and violence—especially in some parts of x-Yugoslavia and x-USSR). There is no space to work except in the space of the political. On the one hand there is the political establishment and writers/editors who are the protagonists of dominant poetical and cultural trends (the glorification of the patriarchal and the mythic consciousness; in art national-realism is the dominant style with new real-socialism as critique of communist society). On the one hand, there are those who are against the political establishment, who are for civil options and values (international values against local values). In both cases, working with culture implies explicitly working in politics. There is no way to work in the field of culture without working in the space of politics. Today, the major figures on both sides (official and oppositional) are mostly the same people who were, in communism, representatives of communist ideology and politics. The same people are still in the game of distribution of political and cultural powers. They were major figures in communist society and they are still major figures now. The question is how cultural models reproduce themselves and how they change in new circumstances when the major protagonists of both culture and politics are mainly the same people? And where is there a place for those who have an explicit political attitude, but do not want to manipulate and instrumentalize their political beliefs and functionalize them in order to get more cultural power?

4. In the patriarchal society in which I live, there are very few women editors. There are also few women critics. But some of the best poets are women. Women poets often do not like their work to be called feminist—feminist in patriarchal society means marginal and without value. As a critic I use methods of feminist discourse to interpret mainly women's writing. I do this so as to examine how poetic discourse (written by women or by men) questions dominant patriarchal models of the culture—does it parody it, destroy it or show its mechanisms, or, on the contrary, does it conform it. My (liberal) male colleagues back up this method; they find it amusing (!) I suppose. The model of poetic discourse reveals the broader model of ideology and with these criteria I want to see what the model

of the ideology of poetic discourse represents (i.e. in the end, what political values does it represent: does it glorify war or not; does it embody patriarchal values or not; does it examine the status and function of the woman and man in society or not?).

5. In post-communist society, which shows an unambiguous tendency towards the totalitarian model of life, writing and editing should have the goal of protecting the necessity of pluralism, multiculturalism, and difference in life and culture.

Dubravka Djuric co-edited issues number three and four of *Mental Space*, an alternative magazine for art.

Johanna Drucker

My one experience of working with women in a project where I served as editor was at least as fraught with problems as any other project—if not more so—though my editing experiences have been few and far between. Not my métier. But I did co-edit an issue of *Raddle Moon* with Susan Clark. The project started with great optimism and enthusiasm on my part, at least. I had had conversations with a number of very interesting women writers I know/knew as friends at the time—Jean Day, Abby Child, Chris Tysh, Susan Clark. It seemed like a good idea to formalize some of the issues we had talked about in person as a project. But as the project developed, instead of sisterhoodly exchange, there was only paranoia, jealousy, and weirdness. In other words, the fact that they were all women maybe even made things worse because there was more identification—less capacity for distance/difference between/among us.

So, gender played a role, but not, as I had hoped, in a positive way.

Also, we never got to the "editing" stage. Communications broke down and Susan Clark took the project to completion so that I didn't, ultimately, participate in giving it a final shape in any editorial sense.

As for women's writing in academia, that story changed fifteen years ago. Tenure policies haven't, but publishing has. The clubbiness and insider/outsider stuff stays in place, but women play the same games as the men once in power. I probably do too, probably am perceived that way at least. Even unintentionally.

I guess I don't see an identity for myself as an editor, at least not for now. It's a bit like being a moderator—I think I prefer just to do my own work.

Ana Maria Fagundo

1. *How does editing influence your work?*

Because I am a poet I founded *Alaluz* in 1969, a journal of poetry and narrative in Spanish. The journal publishes essays about poets, original poems, short stories, book reviews and studies about the works of contemporary women novelists, dramatists and artists. Although Spain's and Latin America's writers are the main focus of the journal, special issues have been dedicated to Women Poets of the Americas (including the USA).

Editing is a rigorous work that takes up much of my time but has also kept me abreast of the literary production in Spanish.

2. *Does gender play a role in your editorial practice?*

Way before gender, feminine writing, etc., became so fashionable, I had been publishing in *Alaluz* as many women writers as men writers. The reason for doing so then and now is, simply, that male writers can be as good as female writers but men have had more opportunities because they had enjoyed for centuries (and still do to a large extent) economic and social privileges that women did not have.

Yes, in this sense gender plays a role not only in my editorial practice but also in my profession: in equal conditions I always vote for women.

3. *Editing as power or subversion.*

Women editors can and should help with the publication of good writing by women.

4. *What obligations do you answer to as an editor?*

I do just about everything: invite writers, artists, and critics, select the texts, mail the journal, take care of the finances, answer the correspondence. Lately, I have had help in handling the subscriptions.

6. *In what ways do you see women's writing surfacing in academic publications which have traditionally been vehicles for men's writing?*

Slowly but surely, women are getting to the power structure of men but the struggle is a hard, very hard one. Nonetheless, conscientious women editors can play a good part in helping women scholars and writers to break through the system and give their own perceptions of things.

7. *How have issues in current feminist theory influenced your editorial practice?*

I have placed even more importance on the presence of women scholars and writers in my journal although they were always there from the very beginning.

Heather Findlay

I have only been the editor of *On Our Backs* for six months—in fact, since I used to be a graduate student in English, I've only been in the publishing business for six months—so I've been spending a lot of time getting my bearings.

Your questions seem to revolve around the question of gender and editing. The first thing that comes to mind for me is the huge difference I've experienced between working in a male dominated institution (academia), versus a small, woman-owned business where most of the employees are lesbians. I've had to assume a position of responsibility without the guidance and/or interference of the authority figures who, when I was a student/T.A., were predominantly straight men. I have found this incredibly frightening and liberating at once. In terms of day-to-day work relations, my labor has been much less individual and isolated, and much more cooperative. Although we are not a collective, my staff (which consists of a designer and an assistant) and I work very closely generating ideas for copy and layout. I am the boss, but I can count on one hand the times that I've laid down any sort of fiat. And then, if any difficulties arise from my decisions, my staff helps me revise them.

Since many of our contributors are not experienced or well established writers, I work very tightly with them during the editing process, gauging their intent and helping them express their ideas more successfully. In fact, meetings with contributors often resemble office hour sessions I used to have with young writers when I was a T.A. Gender has a lot to do with this, because both my contributors and I are unwilling or unable to assume the inflexibility that—for good reason—is stereotypically associated with male writers. This has to do as well with the fact that, since we are a small magazine with limited resources, and since we are part of the lesbian political movement, most of our contributors work with us for recompense that is primarily ideological, not monetary.

On Our Backs is a magazine by and for lesbians. It would seem, then, that our editorial policy about what kind of work we accept from whom would be simple. Indeed, up until I came on board, *On Our Backs* only accepted contributions by women about lesbian issues. But recently we have recognized the extent to which lesbian culture has begun to overlap with that of other sexual minorities (gay men and transsexuals, for example), and we have taken this as an opportunity to expand our horizons. I talk about this as "making the magazine more queer." Overall, I have found it very challenging—in a good, productive way—to be editing a magazine that is defined by gender and sexuality (we are a magazine for lesbian women), but which is, at the same time, exploring the very definition of gender and sexuality itself.

Kathleen Fraser

The Jump: Editing HOW(ever)

Perhaps the most perplexing—and dogged—question submitted to *HOW(ever)* (during my tenure as Publisher & Editor 1983-1991) was often posed as a demand in public forums, as if there existed a conceptualized and certified answer, as if such an answer were desirable, even essential. It went like this: "What kind of work are you interested in publishing?" [Or, to read it another way: What do you approve of or disapprove of? What do you like and dislike?]

There was, at these moments, an attempt by the gentle, determined or accusing interrogator to track what *HOW(ever)* "stood for" aesthetically, to tack down what was wanted, to determine conclusively the basis for our decision to publish a particular poem/work. It continued to puzzle me that the unrehearsable impact of a particular linguistic splicing on the ear and eye (or the musical pressure of vagrant thought) should provoke such insistent need for codification.

It was this casual assumption of a static absolute—as a value—that led me to observe two possible phenomena making their pressure felt in the world of contemporary American writing: 1) a pervasive pragmatics of "buy" and "sell," spawned by a national culture organized around product: who is "buy-ing"/choosing & what shape/size/color is s/he looking for, and 2) a historical but often unconscious habit, perhaps more significant for women, of assuming that literary decisions of consequence were set (carved?) in stone and that their follow through—in publication and critical acclaim—was initiated, articulated and canonized by Male Editors, Critics, Anthologists. Territorial imperative. Case closed.

As late as the mid-Seventies, women still occupied mid-level assistant positions on the mastheads of both commercial and literary publications—acknowledged "first readers" of unsolicited manuscripts, proofers of galleys and keepers of mailing lists, proliferating correspondence, etc. . . .but seldom experienced the pleasure and authority of asserting editorial choices or getting credit for it.

By the Eighties, some things had changed. In May, 1983, when the first issue of *HOW(ever)* went into the mails, "women's writing" had been publicly identified by a group of mostly academic feminist scholar-poets and editors. Their somewhat parochial community agenda focused on:

• the creation of place: (magazine/book/essay/caucus) where women's editorial choices could be asserted & exercised

• the foregrounding of lesbian subjectivity/its literature

• the celebration & legitimization of female body/ "female language" as basic grounds for investigation.

• "common language" (as in Adrienne Rich's *Dream of a Common Langauage* or Judy Grahn's *The Work of a Common Woman*), asserted as the superior agency of literary exchange . . . often seen as the only valid way to empower a female community.

• a growing sensitivity to class/race issues in women's lives

These goals helped to create an important beginning stage for a female-based writing community and its claim to new publishing/editing territory. But for women writers who *resisted* "common language" as a potential replication of the weighty & threadbare treads of the traditional male prosody currently in use (and wary, as well, of prescriptive ideas of "women's poetry"), a taking apart and putting back together of *the poem*—of the very writing process itself—was the exciting task. So much had been hoarded, silenced, pre-Judged as not enough or too much. Shadowing one's masters was no fun.

"Common language" seemed too limited to hold the largesse of female-produced language forms and too essentialist in what it did not express or give value to . . . much like a door slamming and windows clicking shut, the fortress battened down against those who didn't fit the new politically-correct givens of a somewhat single-minded editorial aggregate.

The male power structure we'd learned to recognize and analyze as the basis of the canon-forming profession of literature suddenly had its able female counterpart. This was not any less stifling.

The meaning of inventing *HOW(ever)* in 1983 was absolutely based in the dilemma of and attunement to gender. Our hearts did not belong to Daddy. We believed we could make a place for work that spoke to us and surprised us, without the pressure of producing a BIG, "major" organ. Our goal, instead, was to put together a modest-size publication that adventurous readers—otherwise beseiged by dense work commitments and familial obligations—would feel compelled to read almost immediately.

We hoped that *HOW(ever)* would be a model, not just for a different kind of writing but for the assertion of editorial choices by women. We had no *preconceived esthetic bias*, except that we preferred to be surprised and pulled into linguistic maps that clearly connected us up to sudden locations of self knowledge & recognition of intellectual/spiritual/esthetic zones we might otherwise never have inhabited. We had to trust our individual responses, our discretionary sense of authenticity and difficult pleasure, to acknowledge variable tastes and persuasions as the work began arriving.

We made notes on our reading. Often two of us would love a particular work for which a third would not feel the same enthusiasm. Part of our collective process was to clarify the reasons for our choices, in writing, as an attempt to convince a sceptical or less-than-enthusiastic colleague of the necessity and value of a certain work, to ask for reconsideration when there was a strong difference, to think even more closely about why or how a particular piece was causing excitement in one of us and not in another. We were opening up places that had been shut down by powerful ideas of "worth" and "importance," long circulating through our well-schooled lives.

We never held fast to any policy of total accord, but tried more and more to trust an instinct or conviction in one or another's response, when that intrigue was made sufficiently clear. Through this editorial conversation we educated and provoked one another to continuously widening curiosities and the conciousness of learned prohibitions. Also, our chosen poets helped us with each new work invented as well as with the process-oriented "Working Note" we required with every publication of original work. It was our way into the poet's thinking about the formal problems she'd set for herself—her methods, stimuli, after-thoughts.

On a parallel track with this evolving conversation was the visual esthetic initiated in Vol. I, No. 2, and foregrounded in each issue thereafter, with art works (usually, but not always, by women) focused on alphabets, words, de-composition. Our theme or focus was never determined ahead of time but always emerged from the works chosen, located in the structural underpinnings of that particular converging, inscribed during a discrete time frame. In this way, we avoided predictability because both language and visual image were in a continual process of suggesting each other. Our task was to attend.

I found that my real editorial freedom (what kept me plugging through exhaustion and financial disaster), was the clearing of space for unmapped female experience and formal investigation . . . writing as different in its goals and its "product" as a painting by Nancy Spero or Elizabeth Murray was from a picture by William DeKooning or David Salle. What we were looking for was that which had not yet been uttered because forms were still being imagined to contain these unsayables.

Such a delicate, tricky staging of vulnerability, chanciness and resistance to male editorial approval was the core meaning of our project and in this sense *HOW(ever)*'s gender exclusivity made every difference. We didn't have the pressure of fathers, lovers, favored male poets and teachers from whom we'd learned so much. Whether we could have pulled down grant money, made a bigger academic splash, produced a bigger, slicker product (as one serious male poet advised us, in print, we must do) was vastly beside the point.

Because we *didn't* have to carry all that baggage and hustle, inevitably part of "big," officially funded projects *approved by committee*, we were free to figure out, issue by issue, what fascinated us and drove us to the next cone of attention. It is probably realistic to speculate that even as many male writers were extremely supportive of our undertaking, had any one of them been an active voice in our collective editorial labors, a discretely different sum "product" would have emerged. There would have been a more heavily-weighted set of histories to stare down, a male style of logic and argument with its confident and enlightened pressures always there to negotiate.

In truth, it was exhilirating to hold our collective nose and jump. Every issue felt like a huge risk—up to the final, two-woman proofing . . . and a miraculous if tentative voicing of female presence, just waiting to cut loose.

In retrospect, the one problem I grappled with over the entire course of *HOW(ever)*'s tenure was the issue of women vs. critically reflective writing. My second goal for *HOW(ever)* had been to elicit a set of writings from both established feminist scholars *and* working poets that would elucidate a modernist and current writing practice of apparently such imagined unfamiliarity in women's poetry that it seemed to cause a kind of shut-down mechanism in not only the Male Critics but in the majority of women critic/scholars we looked to for "readings" of our work. They were brave enough to puzzle through Joyce and Woolf, Beckett and Ashbery, but when it came to the "odd" diction or unfamiliar visual forms proposed by a woman poet, the silence was appalling . . . a non-response, I might add, deeply discouraging to writers of immense gifts and proven seriousness.

I hoped that, given an *unofficial* venue, women poets might be able to provide a precise and non-prefabricated description of their intentions and working methods to women critic-scholars, thus enhancing a cross-fertilization among the two arts/disciplines within a "safe" and benevolent framework, unthreatened by any real or perceived form of canonical harassment or institutional bullying. I envisaged, as well, a place for informal, incomplete response to current and historic works, with particular emphasis on recovery of texts, letters, critical reputations of lost or dimming modernist women writers.

The poets we published were instantly implicated in this effort by the "Working Note" required of each. But beyond this, it was the most difficult task to lure anyone into something speculative, partial, "informal," i.e. not sanctioned by the fully-developed, footnoted format. I sent out a large number of personal letters of friendly invitation to feminist scholars and essayists whose work I discovered in my reading. We handed out flyers at regional and national MLA sessions and at conferences on H.D. and E.D. and V.W., inviting contributions . . . but with mostly silence in return.

The poets were the best at taking the jump: to begin to talk about new writing springing out of this quirky, unofficially recognized realm involved the development of a new descriptive language. It became clear that the internalized voice of a male-dominant academic method (and pleasure) of discourse was a fearsome gauntlet yet to be detoured.

The challenge is still there.

HOW(ever) Associate Editors included Frances Jaffer (1983-89), Beverly Dahlen (1983-85); Susan Gevirtz (1985-89). Contributing Editors were Rachel Blau duPlessis and Carolyn Burke (1983-89). Guest Editors for Vol. VI, Nos. 1-3 (1989-90), were Myung Mi Kim and Meredith Stricker. The final issue, Vol. VI, No.4 (Jan. 1991), was again edited by K.F. Special thanks is here given to Susan Gevirtz whose invaluable editorial and emotional support made the editing of *H(er)* a more positive labor.

Susan Gevirtz

Doctor Editor

> Though one may say that I have told nothing new, the
> arrangement of the material is my own.
>
> — Pascal

Shaking Hands

Once the poem is sent, it becomes the patient under the eye of
the Doctor Editor.

> *The illness "discovered" through the interview is constructed, not
> found. A diagnosis is a way of interpreting and organizing obser-
> vations. It is no less real because it is critically dependent on what
> physicians ask and what they hear and on what patients report
> and do not report than it would be if it were based on the results
> of physical examinations and laboratory tests. Since the discovered
> illness is, in this sense, partly a function of the talk between a
> patient and a physician, the study of this talk is central to our
> understanding . . . .*
>
> *(Mishler, 11)*

Every poem is potentially ill. The poem arrives, and the
Doctor meets it in her or his office. The meeting is usually
without witness, without audience. The Doctor must learn
from the patient why she or he has come. This is not a sociable
relationship and yet it has a protocal:

> *1. When meeting a new patient in your office, would you shake
> hands with him?*

> *Answer: Social handshaking occurs primarily when two men meet
> initially or when they have been apart for some time. Shaking
> hands is much less frequent among women. As a social custom,
> shaking hands is not as prevalent in the United States as it was
> 50 Years ago, or as it now is in Europe. Shaking hands in a
> physician's office is not common. After all, it is not a sociable
> relationship. From another outlook, some valuable information
> can be obtained from the handshake (whether the hand is limp or*

firm, wet or dry, steady or shaking, clumsy or agile, deformed or normal). The only rule is to shake hands if it is the comfort- able thing to do *for you and the patient.*

(Froelich and Bishop, 11-12)

The second the physician lays hands on the poem, diagnosis begins. Is the poem deformed or normal, in need or replete, shaky, sweaty, and where does it fall in a range between illness and health? These are the kinds of questions that the poem may elicit from the Doctor Editor. In the initial moments of the interview, even the author's name may shape the nature of contact. It may suggest the bodily contours or color of an imagined author and determine which social customs follow. As a consequence, it may or may not be comfortable to shake hands.

Since the discovered illness is partly a function of the talk between the editor and the writing, the extent to which the Doctor Editor engages in a *study of this talk is central to our understanding.* Whether or not the Doctor Editor takes a double watch, attending to her or his own method of organizing observations (and thus constructing the writing in hand) and at the same time listening closely to the report of the poem, will have significant impact.

Patient Utterances

> *The fact that psychic processes may lead to somatic symptoms, . . . lays upon the physician a special responsibility in regard to his behavior toward the patient. . . . First of all he must remember that his every utterance and act, as well as every therapeutic measure, has a suggestive effect on the patient, only too often of a harmful nature.*
>
> (Dunbar, 349)

Illness or health is "discovered" through a conversation that may occur between the poem and the editor — but, what is the patient? The writer or the poem or the talk between the poem and the editor? And who is the editor? The one who is perpetually in a state of diagnosis, or the one who has gnosis? The kinds of questions asked will also determine what counts as a poem, the condition discovered in it — even whether illness and health are at issue.

1. Several examples of questions that will yield "no" answers of unknown meaning are as follows:
   A. Have you been sick before?
   B. Do you kick Your dog?
   C. Do you smoke excessively?
2. Rewrite the following questions so that they do not suggest the answers.
   A. Has the pain gone into your left arm from your chest?
   B. May I assume you have taken the medicine as directed?
   C. Before taking the medicine do you always try to relieve the pain by resting?

                      (Froelich and Bishop, 33-34)

Does the act of interpretation also become an object of investigation for the Doctor Editor — or is the Doctor Editor in an ice cream parlor choosing his or her favorite flavor? Taste is made from favorite flavors:

      Like chocolate   even vanilla

chocolate   strawberry   sasparilla

         Flavors are electric

               try to get a shocker

         (from "Cold Lampin With Flavor" Public Enemy)

Are favorite flavors learned or genetically inherited?
What profile, mug shot, bust, portrait, composite, does taste take on the page?

Adjuvant Data

The patient's narrative may be assisted, prevented or perverted. Other options may exist if adjuvant data are sought or imagined:

   Adjuvant data are supporting information available to the physician about his patient. Examples are the patient's posture, behavior, style of dress, voice quality, and modulation and the physician's own reactions to the patient.

                      (Froelich and Bishop, 57)

The patient is not a neutral zone.

Now it sometimes happens that a belief . . . transforms itself into a memory. (Auyer, in Coulehan and Block, 55) And then, "taking" a case becomes an act of remembering the patient's past for the patient. Who is hungry for the past? The Doctor may mistake the traditions of the past for her or his present opinion. The Editor who does not seek adjuvant data is at the mercy of her or his beliefs.

The Ward and the Word

> *The perspective of a Person in the scientific attitude is that of a "disinterested" observer. Events in the world are not viewed within subjective coordinates of space and time, but with reference to abstract, standard, and context-free coordinates of "objective" space and time. Events and actions receive their meaning from their location in a general scheme or model from which pragmatic motives have been removed. Interest in the world is theoretical.*
> *(Mishler, 122)*

The recent history of the Doctor and that of the Editor collide in psychoanalysis. Psychoanalysis — the method of interpretation that discovers "the woman question." And Freud, the Editor Writer of the conversation between the Doctor and the Patient. The "woman question" is one question among many possible other questions, that can provide a historical location for thinking about the diagnostic nature of the editorial act. Since events and actions receive their meaning from their location, pragmatic motives can only be traced through material context. *Interest in the world* can then be more and less than *theoretical.*

If the profile of the writing is difficult to decipher, too 'easy,' or eludes diagnosis entirely, the Doctor Editor might decide to do further research on the historical conditions out of which the writing arises. In this hypothetical case Dr. Editor will begin research on the historical locations of his or her own modern origins and the coinciding cultural conditions in which early twentieth-century British and American women writers found themselves. These writers inherited the predominantly white and middle class debate around "the woman question."

With a large increase of women writing in the nineteenth-century one of the main issues around which the "woman question" debates revolved was women's proper relation to writing and literature. These discussions, rampant in medical journals, psychoanalytic discourse, the popular press, and elsewhere, focused on the links between sexuality and art:

> In [mid-nineteenth-century] discussions of women and literature, the sexually laden language suggests two theories. According to one, female imagination is a volatile and highly erotic force that must be repressed or at least controlled; according to the other, women's writing is a sign of sexual and emotional frustration. Both must be seen against the prevailing assumption that artistic creation is, like the sexual act, a male activity in which women have only an extremely restricted part. As the Saturday Review reminds readers in 1865, "Female nature, mental as well as physical, is essentially receptive and not creative."
>
> (Helsinger, et al, 16)

From the mid-to-late Victorian period there was a remarkable increase of madness, of institutionalization and of publication among women. At that time, and on into the early twentieth century, the contradictory demands and expectations on women to be, in the midst of an increasingly industrialized society, representatives of "feminine" purity and order, and to be perfectly controlled in their conduct and skilled in domestic managerial capacities, coincided with a growing fear of female sexuality. (Bernheimer and Kahane, 5)

Freud's main investigation of issues related to the "woman question" centered on his studies of hysterics, almost all female. (Bernheimer and Kahane, 1) As a result of his research, one of Freud's many observations was that, "The mechanism of poetry is the same as that of hysterical phantasies." (Bernheimer and Kahane, 10-11) Freud is useful to this discussion not only as one of the most famous Doctor Editors of this century, but also because his work voiced many of the obsessions and anxieties prevalent in the late-Victorian, early-modernist moment. And so, the conditions and consequences of many of Freud's formulations can be seen as symptomatic of widespread cultural views. For example, in the above formulation all poetry is potentially coded "hysterical" and "feminine." In the larger culture this code presented an at least double problem for women writers who already dangerously occupied the realm of the monstrous in their display of inappropriate excess, manifest in the desire to write, and their excited imaginations evident in the writing itself. According to the "woman question" debates, it was implied, and sometimes prescribed, that women who wrote or did anything "creative," must be controlled by husbands, doctors, or institutions. A writing woman, or a woman who was active in any realm, contradicted her "nature" by being a "creative" agent rather than a passive and receptive container.

While it is true that poetry, like the hysteric, was symbolically coded feminine in the dominant cultural discourse of late-Victorian, early-modern Europe and the United States, some hysterics were actually male, though symptoms of hysteria were often differently diagnosed when observed in male patients, and many poets were, of course, men. The gendering of poetry as feminine in the dominant cultural discourse required of many male poets a defensive stance: some felt the need to demonstrate that they were emphatically not feminine, not mentally or physically ill, that while a man's poetry might partake of the mechanism of hysterical phantasies, he did not. *(For background on all of the above see Burke, 1985; especially 43-47, and Burke 1987.)*

This foray into a turn-of-the-century context and history, however radically truncated, hopefully suggests what might be at stake, and what might be missed or overlooked, in the diagnostic editorial conversation if adjuvant data is not sought. Since diagnostic judgments occur in and are artifacts of the network of cultural discourses that exist at the historical moment in which the editor or doctor lives, and the tradition in which she or he was trained, diagnoses are never neutral — but are always results of inherited and inhabited assumptions. Although taste may not change as a result of the editor's further research, diagnosis may at least become a more complicated act.

Types of Errors

It would be an error to think that the woman question debates have ended.

It would be an error to think we are not all inheritors.

As medical students we make many errors in evaluating patients . . . One kind of mistake arises from your own lack of knowledge of what is known, or culpable ignorance.

(Coulehan and Block, 103)

It would be an error to think you have finished imagining your own history.

In *The Discourse of Medicine*, Mishler says that one of the main elements and dangers of the medical interview is the "process of selective attention on the physician's part." He goes on to say,

> He [the physician] responds to one element of the patient's account, usually her mention of a specific symptom, abstracts it from the context in which it is presented, and then refers to the symptom within another context expressed in the voice of medicine. The symptom is thus transformed by being relocated to a different province of meaning . . . much is lost in the translation from one voice to another. It is as if a poem in one language that uses qualities of the weather, such as its dampness or coldness, as a metaphor for the feeling state of the narrator were to be translated literally into another language as a description of the weather.
>
> (Mishler, 123-24)

Selective attention is a universal phenomenon. And if you have ever tried to pack for the tropics while snow falls outside your window, you know that the editor's weather condition usually becomes the only season and place of reference. All other narrative positions and climatic zones are theoretical.

Face to Mask Interaction

> Although two persons are talking to each other in the medical interview, it does not have the essential reciprocity feature of ordinary face-to-face interaction and might more precisely be viewed as face-to-mask interaction.
>
> (Mishler, 124)

When I was a Doctor Editor on *HOW(ever)*, I found out again how present the turn-of-the-century is in the late twentieth-century. Without access to that history, gestured at above, I would not have known that many reactions to *HOW(ever)* were riddled with the tones and obsessions of the woman question debates.

My recognition of the acute presence of this history in the present was most powerfully triggered when we received a copy of a review of *HOW(ever)* Vol. I, No. 4 (May 1984) by Robert Peters. In the last paragraph of his review Peters says,

> *I have yet to meet anyone who has been able to sit and read Gertrude Stein for more than one hour at a stretch (Kenneth Rexroth alone has had the balls to say so in print), or to remain excited by H.D. after twenty pages or so. These seem the primary goddesses behind this sort of writing. A poem is not a dictionary. A poem is not a set of easy metaphysical speculations on the nature of grammar, guilt or the primal flood. . . . Let's not keep the trope flying let's strangle the little creature in his crib before he soils his pants and screws up our life.*

The infant poem in the above paragraph, like the baby in a crèche scene, brought into sharp focus in a diorama, is the alive-and-well embodiment of high anxiety about women's relation to writing in our own cultural midst. The infant poem (above) is a recalcitrant, necessarily male, "creature." The poem is male since, in this framework, it would be impossible to imagine a poem as anything but an adored son — even if the mechanism by which he enters the world is hysterical phantasy via an unnatural and dangerous goddess. This infant — a result of excess, and himself excessive (like a dictionary) and boring (after twenty pages or so) might, if not strangled first, return as trope, to spread excrement all over the clean white sheets of the page and "screw up our life."

Their Life, composed of a Victorian cleanliness and order, the life that the Doctor Poet in the above paragraph shares with his medical colleagues, is a life without ambiguity. Its flavor is vanilla, its crime is metaphysical speculation. Balls in print are its mascot. In this world a poet knows what a poem is and is not, and she who produces "this sort of writing," should beware of strangulation.

Resources

Bernheimer and Kahane, editors, *In Dora's Case Freud-Hysteria-Feminism.* New York: Columbia U P 1985.

Burke, Carolyn, "Getting Spliced: Modernism and Sexual Difference." *The American Quarterly*, 39:1, Spring, 1987.

____.The New Poetry and the New Woman: Mina Loy," in *Coming to Light: American Women Poets of the Twentieth Century.* Eds. D. Middlebrook and M. Yolom. Ann Arbor: U of Michigan P, 1985.

Coulehan, John L. and Marian R. Block. *The Medical Interview: A Primer for Students of the Art*. Philadelphia: F.A. Davis Company, 1987.

Dunbar, Helen Flanders. *Emotions and Bodily Changes*. New York: Columbia U P, 1946.

Engel, George L., and William L. Morgan. *Interviewing the Patient*. London: Saunders Company Ltd, 1973.

Froelich, Robert E., and Bishop, Marian F. *Medical Interviewing: A Programmed Manual*. Saint Louis: The C.V. Mosby Company, 1972.

Helsinger, Sheets and Veeder. *The Woman Question*. New York: Garland, 1983.

Mishler, Elliot George. *The Discourse of Medicine: Dialectics of Medical Interviews*. Ablex Publishing Corporation, 1984.

Peters, Robert, "*HOW(ever)*." I have been unable to locate the place of publication for this article. It was xeroxed and mailed to us by a male poet.

Showalter, Elaine, *The Female Malady, Women, Madness and English Culture, 1830-1980*. New York: Penguin, 1985.

I was an associate editor on *HOW(ever)* from 1985-1989. See the note at the end of *HOW(ever)* editor Kathleen Fraser's essay, included in this collection, for the editorial history of *HOW(ever)*. I remain in gratitude to Kathleen Fraser and all who participated in the *HOW(ever)* project as writers and editors. And to the legacy of that community, in which I, and so many women writers now live.

Jessica Grim

Editorial Forum—*Big Allis*—Notes

I've set out many times in the last weeks to respond to this query, and each time I seem to be working towards expressing a different set of thoughts about this act of editing. We've never published an editorial statement, introductory notes, or announcement of intent. The magazine's been left to "speak for itself." Of the six issues of *Big Allis* published, two issues have included work only by women; in the other four issues, collectively, we've published the work of 37 women, and 16 men. This bias obviously reflects our editorial tastes and interests (as does our bias towards formally innovative work); it also reflects our very distinct commitment to publishing work by women.

We never expected that the politics of editing, the problems of accepting/rejecting work, the power relationships created would be different/easier/less inevitable simply because we have a commitment to publishing work by women, or, even more absurd, because we are women. Sometimes I feel as though we don't get challenged enough—as if people are hesitant to attack or question a project that appears to be gender-based (though one amusing incident does come to mind—when we were soliciting work for an early issue, it was suggested to us by a male poet that we should not be soliciting work from men because it would compromise the integrity of the magazine— yet he clearly felt there would be no compromise involved in our taking his advice).

Issues and problems of feminism, post-feminism, being pigeon-holed, run a constant parallel to our editorial practice; the extent to which these issues and problems enter in is determined by the work, which ranges from pieces that are clearly cognizant of/responding to feminist theory, to work that has no apparent reference to theory at all. The most frightening, and untheoretical, possible future is the continuation of the one where women were seen to be peripheral, secondary, minor writers. We wouldn't have started a project that identified itself as originating from a position of marginality. Whose margin? If you start from the center it stays the center as far as it goes, and seeing how far it goes has been the interesting thing.

It's been great to see the editing projects being taken up by women recently (*Black Bread*, and of course *Chain* are the titles that immediately come to mind). Yet at the same time the specter of a magazine I just received the premiere issue of hovers. In the introduction the editors make claims for the renewal of a spiritually-inclined/informed poetics, and in doing so level nasty, reductive, and untrue charges against the "formalistic avant-garde." That there's a perceived need for this kind of overblown reactionary move is discouraging to me as an editor, an example of an unnecessary inflationary move within the "exchange economy of editorial practice."

Big Allis was founded by Melanie Neilson and Jessica Grim in 1989. Six issues have been published. *BA* is available through Small Press Distribution, and is $6 per issue.

Barbara Henning

"The Editorial We"

1984. Six hundred and ninety-eight miles from the Cass Corridor, homesick. In a bar on Cortelyou Rd, two ex-Detroiters. Nostalgia weaves over, around and through the depressive void. Construction worker prose, a glossy quarterly, hard-boiled experimental writing. I-80 with easy Miles angling computer, postal, library, telephone lines. Back in Brooklyn: You're too theoretical. You're too realistic. Romance as a pornographic photo slipped under the bedroom door. One again. A call from Cincinnati. Tell the truth, but tell it long. The New York School of non-regional (in love) writing. Over breakfast, lunch and dinner, belief in one's ELF. If I ever sell out (shut up in an educational pamphlet) let me know—

1990. You glue. The children asleep. Every ten pages, hiero-glyphic relief. 5th Street at Second Avenue. I'll type Michigan, France, California, the Lower East Side. Everyday arrange-ments. Writers writing writers. London, Washington D.C., New Orleans. Toy soldiers on a broken phonograph. (The Gulf War.) Two dogs, four cats, four children, two mothers. (A low cash balance.) Ten cases of paper. (A guilty conscience.) After that, Montreal. (Institutional politics to the grass.) Take it to the bindery. Take this poem to the Café and read it outloud. (Cross the expanse of the lawn.) Together, we work well. (He won't speak to me on the street when we pass.) Bookmaker. Why did you move that photograph to the back of the book? Can't you be patient? (The spine is upside down.) He's suddenly so friendly. (Homeless.) Why are you speaking in such an irritated tone? (HIV positive.) A note in the mail. (The Berlin Wall.) For god's sake, why did you publish him? (An inability to mourn.) Of course, I like your writing. I'd never send anything to such an academic journal (though).

1993. Do you realize how many times you've called me today? I'm trying to quit smoking and we're moving into a new house. I haven't been able to spend more than one hour this week on my own work. (The liberties of interruption.) I hate this maga-zine. No funding this year. Merely unlikely, but not impossible that he would write something beyond the ethics of arousal. I situate my work between both genders. (The body has been the center.) I'm not charming. I liked your earlier work. I like Edgar Allan Poe. I hate this genre. Lacan is not a god to me. *I am saddened by all this.* (Because I am afraid.)

Today you're an editor. *I'm nobody. Who are you?* Aim for eight. I can't understand three words he writes. What a lovely section. Keep that philosophy coming. I loved the last issue of Long News. To be honest, I didn't understand more than two pages in this entire book. What's the point? So glad you took my advice. (The necessity of interruption.) Told a friend to send you something. (You always go out with such aggressive women.) The men come in envelopes (send me a poem). The women hesitate. More often with an arm in the door. One on top of the other. Task-oriented. With no inner life. (One man to the next: She's difficult at times, but we'll mold her.) Is it necessary, for the final touch, to soar, even with the tip of my thumb sliced off. Even with the tip of yours. To gather toward the 80%. The necessary fights. (You get along with men better.) To be able to read and say: This is it. (Women are like that.) "No" is the wildest word around. To arrange and present. To orchestrate. To refuse to budge.

Long News: In the Short Century. Editor: Barbara Henning Art Editor: Miranda Maher. Contributing Art Editors: Rick Franklin and Sally Young. Contributing Literary Editors: Don David, Michael Pelias, Chris Tysh, Lewis Warsh, Tyrone Williams. Guest Editor: Charles Wolfe. Address: PO Box 150-455, Brooklyn, New York, 11215. So far, we have published four issues of *Long News: In the Short Century.* The first issue was published in the spring of 1991. Issues will be published annually in the Fall of each year. We focus on new writing, visual art, and theoretical essays that create a bridge between poetics and intellectual writing. The second issue focused on "mourning" as a response to the Gulf War; the fourth issue included a special section as a "Homage to Felix Guattari." The journal is widely distributed, by DeBoer, Small Press and Fine Print; it is available nationally in many bookstores. Subscriptions are available.

Beth Joselow

I used to be the literary editor of *Washington Review* for a few years before I passed the baton to Joe Ross. It was important to me then to be open to well-developed new work and ideas, from whatever quarter, rather than to establish too much of a rigid identity for the magazine. For some people, the magazine was therefore not exclusive enough. I have mixed feelings about that issue as I think that the urge to identify and to strictly mark off one's territory can be detrimental to the growth of ideas, or of a movement. And yet, a magazine or publishing venture has little reason to exist among the many unless it has some kind of identifiable mission.

I also felt that it was pointless to publish negative reviews of books. We received so many more books than we could ever attend to that it seemed a waste of space and time to give attention to books we did not like. Perhaps this was a feminine nurturing instinct at work. But that policy, too, was held up to argument by those who felt that there was little interest in reviews that were always positive. I disagree, feeling very strongly that we must not kill each other off. It's tough enough out there.

I am always drawn to work by women, and to collections of women's work. At the same time, I am dedicated to the idea of mainstreaming everyone in order to more quickly blur the boundaries between us, if that is possible. I'm not sure that it is possible, but I recall how frustrated I felt when my friends were wearing shirts that said, "It's a black thing. You wouldn't understand." I want to. And I want to keep the dialogue open and lively.

Martha King

Considering the questions and/or issues
in your August letter:

I'm afraid I start by being contentious: I'm not sure people really have *gender,* not the way languages do. We have sex. And clearly my sex does a great deal more than influence my work, sex being the first particular anyone notes about us as individuals. That and our "normality" or lack thereof (all the toes, e.g.). "It's a girl." "It's a boy." Bedrock. For all of us, even the exceptions, sex, "normality," and family membership or lack thereof are the first three skeins or grids that imposed an exterior order on the plastic unknown we each were at birth. What happens after that? (A glorious horrible mess.)

I continue to be a somewhat plastic thing, certainly. I have a powerful drive for freedom of action, which informs my mental life, my "style" as a daughter, wife, and mother of daughters—and, very certainly, my intentions as an editor and writer. Does this drive spring from my sex? Not all women share it, so "no" is obvious. Does it have *nothing* to do with my sex? Obviously, "no" because sex is so basic to my identity. But—and here I part company with some people—I do doubt that there is an innately feminine (sex-based) way to think, because nothing else in human nature is that tidy. Even one's degree of right- or left-handedness occupies a position on a gray scale.

What do I do with the politics of sex? current life and times? Very little that is obvious unless one takes my drive for freedom of action as a feminist stance. But doing so in the context of freedom makes the word "feminist" sound exclusionary and restrictive—the very opposite of feminism as I define it.

Yes, I'm a feminist, but I'm not a member of very much at all, to my detriment but for my personal needs. I don't "believe" in being an outsider; I haven't adopted it in pursuit of a theory. It's so for other reasons. Of course, the angle of vision an outsider position gives me can't be separated from my editorial ideas. These attributes—outsider status, feminism, personal needs—ought all to be taken together by anyone trying to "understand" what I do. But I'm not sure if that's essential, or even what you asked, which probably had to do with the ways that feminist *theory* has influenced my outlook. In any event, my attributes aren't virtue, just a set of facts. Because, therefore, thus, etc., I define my obligations as an editor in a certain way; derive rather particular personal pleasures from editing, see the arena as I do and think of editing as a powerful act rather than a service. (Of course it is that too.) And I consider its relationship to feminist theory rather remote.

I started *Giants Play Well in the Drizzle* in 1983 as a personal action against personal boredom and despair. A joy-in-doing, a focus on enlarging work which had seemed so evident among the poets I'd known as a very young woman was a nostalgic memory. Literally, people were dead. The magazines I read felt like dust or dross. Bad time. Bad place. Flat sadness. Loss. 1983.

I don't see time in neatly defined decades. (And there's a reason why that's a game so beloved by the popular news.) Thus I don't mean any of what I'm about to write as statements about some past decade safely in the past—much as I would love to write "we were living in a fascist time." I saw (many people did) ostentatiously expensive magazines—part of the $1500 "work boots," fuck everyone, it ain't cheesy if it's expensive ethic. Then there were magazines and newsheets that were self-consciously manifesto bound, often absorbed in laying down orthodoxies disguised as radical reforms. And a flood of "everything is everything, nothing means anything, everyone is an artist, everything is art" anti-art, anti-idea material. And magazines, books, anthologies, and social groups rigidly arranged by social position, income, lifestyle, and personal association, but commonly claiming race, sex or sexual preference, geography, or national origin as their major selection criterion. And major virtue as well. Everyone had a reason why you weren't to argue with it!

As if that weren't enough, publications were ugly—littered with neon & tv colors, clogged with collage and text-collage assaulting the eyes. Actual reading was often impossible. Or publications proclaimed their expensive production—as an end in itself it seemed. You could read those, but you had to put up with being in $1500 work-boot territory.

Now, I'm no Luddite. The old days weren't so great. At the turn of the century, women who campaigned for the vote were called suffragettes, for god's sake, and the word has been legitimate ever since. In the time I look back on so fondly diminishment was, as usual, a near universal way of the world. The club, or clubs, as usual, uncritically belittled the contributions of non-club members. Membership, as usual, was tight. Later on, group divisions that earlier might have been say, men of European ancestry and Ivy League educations were supplanted by new divisions: say, gay men who are fathers and live on the

West Coast. I recognize the problem of routine belittlement: I'm disappointed at dead-end behavior being taken as a solution.

I felt at that time my pleasures, my rage, my love of freedom, my interests—all were degraded, ignored by poets, of interest only to me, a situation no outsider can live with. And I thought this was my fault, a faulty angle of vision. It couldn't be so, since poets by definition make poetry, and since, like you, I could go back to the first time I got a poem, the head-spinning sensation of it, and remember the discovery that I could go back again and again to that stream of language, that something that hit so right, and read it again—and find more. I tried to imagine what a little vehicle, a zine, cheap as cheap could be, could find to carry in the midst of that bad roar. If I started a magazine, what would I publish? Would I find enough to fill just four pages? six? What if my criterion were simply to publish what I wanted to include, ask only "does it move"? Very basic. Does it remind me of what makes me love poetry? Cold? Heat? Energy?

How very odd that was. It was a form of prayer. I really didn't care who wrote the work I took. Or how I came to obtain it. The sex of the author was not on my mind. Nor if I had heard the person's name or not. If a poem I wanted came over the transom; if I plucked three lines from a manuscript of inchoate raving; if I asked a writer I admired to send me something; if I found something in my reading I wanted to include—I didn't care. Fair use. Once I published a poem I found in a wet paper airplane in the front yard:

> *Class News*
> *Today is Thursday, April*
> *14, 1983. It is a cool*
> *day. The temperature*
> *is 40 degrees and it is*
> *Cloudy. King Kong is*
> *inflated and is standing*
> *on the Empire State*
> *Building.*

Early on, I occasionally lifted from published sources, figuring to claim "fair use" if I were ever challenged. Later, rather soon, really, I had the opposite problem . . . more work that I wanted to use than I had room for (meaning, really, money and time). My little rag, my flag. This led to a certain playfulness in the use of page space (Hello Mallarmé) as I was driven by the best of incompatibles—esthetics and economics. Keep that baby light enough to mail for the minimum rate.

Oh yes, and I carried out my willful theme by simply mailing copies of the magazine to people I thought (hoped) might read it—whether I knew them or not. Stamps were 22¢ then, and giving the magazine away was by far the cheapest, simplest way to circulate. I wouldn't have to bother about subscription records, renewals, labeling codes, or feel uneasy because certain people pay for copies while others get it free, all in the normal way of the world. *Giants* wasn't, in any remote sense, a business.*

For me, there is a great deal more to publishing than selecting work. These ideas are quite independent of selection criteria: I consider an editor's responsibility is primarily *to the publication taken as a whole* and what publication does (or doesn't do) to the texts chosen. The word is "use": a text chosen for publication will be used. Publishing is a powerful act, precisely here, after selection. How the works are hung on the wall becomes the question. How the language is set on the page. In which order, and where. With what space. What is the whole? Where does the page fold? yes, because that changes what the reader will see. How do the sounds flow from one piece to the next and what hangs over? For the dust of one poem is going to spill onto the opening of the next, and this issue is especially critical if texts appearing in the same publication are held together internally in accord with very different systems of order, conception, theory if you will. Laura Riding opposed anthologies altogether, which, of course any magazine is. Her radical intensity speaks to this issue, springs from recognition of these phenomena. So have no part of it, she says. If you followed her reasoning all the way out, all writers would have to be their own printers and publishers. Before ultimate control becomes paramount or I get sidetracked thinking about the beautiful tradition of printer-publisher-poets, a little reality check is in order. Books and magazines aren't time-bound as performances or tapes are, so readers always make their own

---

*Actually, I was initially given the use of the nonprofit bulk-mailing permit belonging to Richard Kostelanetz's Assembling Foundation, for which I thank him—and Mitch Highfill, Greg Succop, and Charles Doria, who that year took a short-lived, brave pass at reconstituting Assembling as a book publisher. For the first two issues, *Drizzle* was a project of Assembling Foundation and I mailed copies for something like 8¢ apiece. Non-delivery of bulk mail was so high, and the zip-code bundling requirements so onerous, I dropped the arrangement.

way through the text, some utterly obedient to narrative or numerical progress, others who skip, skim, and double back and subvert editorial balance. That doesn't change the editorial imperative. It's just a "bear in mind." I'd never refrain from using a word I want because some reader might not know what it means.

This responsibility for bringing the senses together, for conducting or arranging is, in fact, the work and the play of editing. It's the part of the task that is, to some degree at least, budget-free. It's the place where my kitchen-table publication can stand among any others, in the life of the mind, and in the space offered to readers. Does this answer your question about editorial obligations—and whether editing is an issue of economy or aesthetics? I do want to be clear about the power an editor has over work—that it isn't confined to selection—that it's influenced but not wholly constrained by the amount of money one can spend—that, most of all, it is power of a more subtle variety than enough people suppose. If this editorial power were exercised more consciously and understood as a working embodiment of an editor's political/aesthetic convictions, we all might have a lot more fun reading. It could be a lot more interesting. Maybe folks could leave off belaboring paper with announcements of intentions, explanations, and jeremiads. We'd expect to see convictions in action, as it were, informing the experience of reading. We might be free of the sense that there's a cryptic oath of club membership involved sub rosa (or do I mean sub text?). We'd be more aware of the created texture. We'd know the publication always comes from some place. And that it means something that it is here in your hands, even if it floats in, uninvited . . . five pieces of paper fastened with a staple. It's a meta-work.

And an editor might go so far as to hope (I might have done so!) that some writer's work never looked as strong or clear as it did in a particular publication. Or that connections not commonly assumed were available for discerning readers. Or that space was enlarged, and if a sense of chorus was implied, it wasn't limited to singing in unison.

How different editing is from the work of making a text myself! I happened to think no one—not even Basil King—could be so many people. Has editing been an influence on my work? It's been an influence on my life, but you aren't asking for biography. I did hope to complete the *Drizzle* by publishing an anthology, which I imagined as containing everything that ever appeared in the magazine: texts by 279 people over a ten-year period. I'd re-edit the whole, as a book, not by deleting but by arrangement for book reading. I don't know how it would "come out"—only that I would work that out in the working—but I don't think such a project will happen. I can't justify taking on all the slush work required without some hope of actual publication. I suppose I'm feeling my age. A *Drizzle* anthology specs out at about 250 pages, far more money than I could possibly find myself. It might work if I could find some funds to be offered, an emollient, a subsidy to the publisher who would take on such a commitment in paper and production costs. I'd still have to raise the funds and I've got these outsider problems. There's no group whose future well-being would be enriched by this book. I don't fit state or national grant requirements because I mailed the magazine out at my own expense and never pretended to be a business. (I checked all the application regs.) My cup's still out, though, hope in a hat, and I welcome any ideas.

I was and am grateful for all the texts I selected (even the mistakes, and you won't get a list out of me). I'm grateful they were there so I could publish them. (Delightful tautology.) Because my instinct was right. They keep on coming. I didn't enter an exchange economy (as in publish my poems and I'll publish yours) but I did get to read a lot of work I wouldn't have seen otherwise, both submissions, and exchange magazines from here and there. I got a lot of dross, yes. But in a bad time, and from sometimes terrible places, there were texts to publish, texts that did, that do, all the things. Made me giggle or freeze, feel puzzlement, surprise, challenge, distress, delight, recognition, curiosity, revulsion. Also, in a very rare while, blue transcendence. Ah. This exchange greatly influenced my other work, and my life, and makes me know I'll inevitably enter into another editorial practice. Perhaps soon. I wonder what?

Avis Lang

A Few Personal Paragraphs

It is now seventeen years since the first issue of *Heresies* appeared. Its triple-edged theme, "Feminism, Art and Politics," has been the reference point, the territory of each of the twenty-seven issues we've managed to produce. I say "we" because *Heresies* really has been a collective all these years, never the platform or the fiefdom of one or two women; since mid-1989 there has been a part-time managing editor, but never an editor with control over content. And I say "managed" because the collective process that gives birth to each issue (sometimes after gestations of three, four, even five years and often involving multiple changes in the roster of participants) is never a well-oiled, efficient, pragmatic experience. Often it feels as though we are reinventing the wheel. Nonetheless, the magazine has survived and, I believe, retained a recognizable character that results from many minds and hands always having been involved in the decision making.

In my four years as managing editor, a job that also involved doing the work of an executive director, the organization faced many difficulties: a necessary, time-consuming, and repugnant lawsuit against a former office manager; disagreements about accepting NEA funds; deep cuts in our usual funders' budgets; the need to repopulate the main collective after many of the first- and second-generation members decided to return to their studios and desks; deep cuts in the discretionary funds of our typical subscribers. I very much wanted *Heresies* to survive; I remembered buying the first issue at a Women's Caucus for Art conference in February 1977, thinking the magazine was fabulous, assigning articles to my students. But survival at any cost? No. Only survival as continuity. Preservation of collectivity seemed essential.

During my tenure only three issues were published. A fourth was underway when I left (I completed it free-lance so as to have the satisfaction of finishing what I'd begun). I may have been very wrong, but I didn't fight the enormous delays; not only were they caused in part by our obvious problems, they also seemed in part inevitable, a given of alternative, noncommercial publishing. I came to feel that when good people are working on a volunteer or near-volunteer basis, you simply cannot push them if you want their best efforts—especially if they want to put forth their best efforts. And since there was no shortage of printed matter being produced all around us, I also came to feel that the only thing that could distinguish *Heresies* from the many other anthologies and magazines that used much spiffier paper and had color reproductions besides would be (dare I use this antediluvian, dangerous word?) excellence, and that *Heresies* wasn't worth bothering with if we put deadlines ahead of a sense of care about editing and design. Careful editing means fixing, pruning, correcting, and nudging someone's writing until it is as strong, as devoid of missteps, and, in its own terms/style/idiom/voice, as right as it can be. The managing editor for a mainstream publisher owned by a food-processing conglomerate might discourage the $12-an-hour copy editor from suggesting anything beyond correction of massive errors. But at *Heresies* I filled both slots and could therefore give myself the satisfaction of reading and rereading the selections until I could inhabit each author's head; then either reworking or simply polishing them; sending corrected manuscripts to and conferring with authors; checking translations, spelling, and diacritical marks; and proofreading more than once. I also made sure the designer had an equal chance to do her best (within the parameters of b&w pages, ordinary 60 lb. paper, and two-color cover). The less money the publishers of the alternative press have to spend, the more important it becomes to create a space that allows skilled people to achieve the excellence they're capable of; besides working toward a better world, getting a chance to be creative, "prestige," experience, and/or friendship, there are few reasons to put up with the difficulties of working on a shoestring.

A final comment: Since the mid-1970s I have worked on, volunteered for, taught in, curated, and written about various women-only or women-centered projects and contexts. I thoroughly enjoyed almost every one of them. I am days away from turning fifty and now no longer gravitate primarily toward such projects. I see too much fragmentation and division around me, too much racial and religious hatred, too much emphasis on the differences among us and not enough on what connects us, too little attention being given to the question of how the people of this planet can manage to live alongside if not with one another. I am tired of questions of identity. Now I intend to take with me into the fray some of the good will, cooperation, and absence of hierarchy I have experienced with the women who are my sisters and see if I can find ways to spread it a little farther afield, out where most of us are still treated badly and where it's less pleasant, but necessary, to be.

HERESIES : *A Feminist Publication on Art and Politics* (P.O. Box 1306, Canal St. Station, New York, NY 10013). Published by Heresies Collective Inc., a nonprofit tax-exempt corporation. Founding collective—20 members. Current collective—18 members. One to two issues are published per year. There is a thematic approach to each issue, e.g., "The Art of Education," "Racism Is the Issue," "Latina—A Journal of Ideas," "Women and Architecture," "Women and Music," "On Women and Violence," "Food Is a Feminist Issue," "Coming of Age," "Feminism and Ecology." The contents of each issue are selected by a different volunteer editorial collective composed of members of the *Heresies* main collective plus other women interested in the particular theme. Upcoming issues: "Women See Men" (1994), "AUTO/BIO/GRAPHY" (1995), "Hair." A four-issue subscription is available for $27 (individuals); $38 (institutions within U.S.). Available by subscription or in bookstores specializing in women's work, art, the alternative press, and the gay/lesbian press, plus some mainstream bookstores. Approximately one third of the subscriptions are held by university and art museum libraries—primarily in the U.S., Canada, England, Australia, and New Zealand but many other countries as well. Modest ongoing General Program Support from Visual Artists Program at New York State Council for the Arts, occasional support from National Endowment for the Arts (although none for the coming year), other recent foundation support from Ms. Foundation for Education and Communication, Inc., The Literature Program of the New York State Council for the Arts, and Soros Foundation.

Holly A. Laird

Editing Feminist Journals: Report on the October 1993 Conference, "Publishing Feminist Scholarship"

On October 30, 1993, a conference on "Publishing Feminist Scholarship" was sponsored by the *NWSA Journal* and directed by its editor, Patrocinio Schweickart, for editors of feminist journals. There are more than one-hundred feminist journals, listed in indexes like that of *Feminist Periodicals*, and one-fifth of them—twenty-one journals altogether—were represented by editors at the University of New Hampshire last fall. Feminist editors have met before on panels, of course, but as far as I know, this was the first conference devoted to their concerns, and so it was an exciting moment for its participants. Would it be the threshold to a new period of greater exchange and collaboration among feminist journals? What would the discussions themselves yield: what divisions would break the editors' ranks, what would seem unresolvable, what would be their agreements, what would be their plans? These were only the most obvious questions, and they were too large, the day itself too short to come fully to terms with them. In facing each other, we could count on the (as indeed it seemed) enormous common ground of feminist purpose, but as it turned out, we also had to come to grips with a wide range of differences in editorial management, procedure, and aim. Moreover, each of us encountered in the others her own impermanence: many of us representing journals which had just begun, several of us representing a short moment in a journal's history and already looking forward to succession by others to the editorial role, still others not present at all as a result of the usual constraints on feminist journals—small budgets, little time, and endless deadlines. In the end, we reached agreement on the simplest of practical measures: first, that we would meet again, and second, that we would go on-line with a feminist editors' bulletin board.

Cheap, fast, and astoundingly open to conversational exchange, electronic publishing could do much to facilitate the production of feminist scholarship and collaboration, and so the establishment of "femedit" is a particularly important first step toward those goals, though it remains up to those it serves to make of it what they will. It was the birth of "femedit" that encouraged my hope of developing a "chain" of our thoughts on feminist editing (emerging out of the conference) for the forum proposed by *Chain*. The chain that has emerged is a short one: no more than six "links" reached me in time for the deadline (and only one of those by e-mail; we remain wedded to print and paper). What follows, then, is a chain of my own thoughts on feminist editing as prompted by the six links I received and the October conference.

Some of these thoughts bear directly on the questions proposed by *Chain* for this forum, others indirectly. The question, "does gender play a role in your editorial practice?" was, for us, a rhetorical question: yes, it does, and yes, it must. As to the issue of "Editing as power or as subversion of power," the assumption was that editing could act as both power and subversion. We tended to shift quickly from the knotty theoretical issues actually at stake in questions such as these, however—or even not to ask the questions at all—to address the practical problems of editing. Yearning for the benefit of each other's experience, seeking tips from each other's experience, we soon became engrossed in the "how to" of editing rather than in the "why." Yet this is itself an issue, not only for feminist editors, but for editors generally: the consumption of editors' minds, skills, and energies by the mechanical details of journal processes.

Too often I have seen "practical" constraints become artificial limits to rethinking a policy. "To think" about journal editing becomes to describe "what we [already] do." The editor seems powerless to do anything but operate the journal, and to do so as efficiently and cost-effectively as possible. Another question raised by the editors of this forum was whether "editing [is] an issue of economy or an issue of aesthetics, or both?" Surely in this case, when practical concerns begin to override other concerns, economic exchange—and the production of a particular aesthetic product to market (whether the "aesthetic" look of eminence in a scholarly journal or the streetsmart look of a newsletter)—becomes editorial policy. In response to my femedit request for thoughts on feminist editing, Ruth-Ellen Joeres, co-editor with Barbara Laslett of *Signs: Journal of Women in Culture and Society*, wrote that

> My impressions of our conference ranged from great pleasure that we were finally meeting to a sense that numbers of other feminist editors should have been there as well. I was struck by the continuous conversation we engaged in, continuous, no

doubt, because some of the problems we discussed (accessibility; too many books to review; financial woes, etc.) are common to most or all of us. At the same time, because we as editors are mostly buried in managing and obviously have to think along those lines, we had too little time for discussing less immediate issues that are also of interest to us, such as how we are perceived nowadays increasingly as "gatekeepers" who might possibly block certain types of feminist scholarship; how we can best represent current debates in feminism, such as the conflicts among feminists in their understanding of what "feminism" should encompass; how we can increase the range of our audiences, both readers and potential contributors. The panels we had were full of useful information that it is important to share, but I hope that as the group becomes more of an established thing, it might find time for some musing, creative, off-the-wall discussions.

But while these feminist editors were captivated by practical problems, they were also acutely aware of why they had become engaged in such practices in the first place, and the procedures they described reflected all the urgency and determination, scrupulousness and complexity of feminist thought. The day began with a talk by Patrice McDermott, author of a forthcoming book on academic journals, on "The Risks and Responsibilities of Feminist Journals," in which, among other things, she urged feminist editors to use—and not flinch from—their powerful roles as academic "gatekeepers." But a number of the editors clearly had other constituencies in mind than that of the tenurable: for example, the editors of *Signs* and *Women's Review of Books* had their sights fixed on an audience stretching beyond the academic marketplace, while the editors of *Gender and History* and *Sex Roles* were focused on vast scholarly audiences and on their roles as revisionary shapers of knowledge.

Replying to my femedit request, Patricia A. Farrant, editor of *Initiatives*, the journal of the Washington-based National Association for Women in Education, struck a very different note from any of these in meditating on her role as editor. She speaks of feminist editing as "mentorship":

> For me, one of the most rewarding—albeit time and energy consuming—aspects of serving as editor of *Initiatives*, has been the numerous opportunities I've had to serve as "mentor unseen" to writers aspiring to publish for a professional audience. Because we are committed to publishing articles on topics that are important to women in higher education but may not yet be receiving the attention they warrant, I often receive manuscripts prepared by people who are new to professional publishing.

I think the process of collecting and analyzing reviewer comments and then developing a thoughtful, specific, and collegial communication (no terse two liners!) to the author satisfies a vague but ever-present wish to be back on campus, in one-to-one contact with students. Within the time constraints inherent in any essentially volunteer task, I'm committed to working with as many young writers as possible, as they struggle through the whole process of journal publishing, even though it may entail several rounds of revision and refinement. More than a few of the women we've published over the years have told me that successfully placing an article was a key that unlocked their confidence and motivated them to tackle other challenges and take other professional risks.

Thus, I find it especially puzzling that only about half of the authors whom we invite to revise and resubmit actually do so. Given the relative scarcity of mentors for women, it seems shortsighted at best to waste the opportunity to work with unseen mentors—journal editors and manuscript reviewers.

Mentorship is, I believe, both a primary "responsibility" and a potential "risk" (to return to the terms of Patrice McDermott's talk) of the feminist editor: we surely are as responsible to the authors we publish—the producers of our pages—as to the readers we seek, yet in the delicate balance of our multiple responsibilities, mentorship risks upsetting a journal schedule or deflecting energy from maintaining readership. But for most feminist journals, "mentorship" has been built into the journals' foundational practices, for example, through specialist readers and a careful editor at *Initiatives*, through the extraordinary global editorial collective at *Gender and History*, or through the multi-levelled system of specialist and common readers and an editorial board at *Signs*.

The first of three panels at the conference took up the issue of "Academic Accountability and Feminist Politics"; its panelists included Ruth-Ellen Joeres of *Signs* on "The Accessibility of Intellectual Language," Sue Rosenberg Zalk of *Sex Roles* on "The Role of Feminist Journals in the Larger Community," and myself on "Gatekeeping and the Feminist Journal." "Accessibility" seemed to many of these editors as important, in some instances a more pressing responsibility than that of "mentorship." And "theory" was perceived by several editors as a continuing challenge to—and disrupter of—accessibility. Thus Marina Budhos, coordinating editor of *Issues Quarterly*, a new publication of the National Council for Research on Women, explained the aim of her journal (in answering my request for contributions to this femedit report):

In publishing *Issues Quarterly*, the new publication of the National Council for Research on Women, we hope to translate the sometimes opaque and dense materials of academic research on women to a broader audience. Within and without the academic community there has been a growing concern that this research should become more accessible. The work we choose to highlight is research and information that can cut across the divides of professions and that links theoretical concerns with practical applications. Women's Studies journals should also consider a more consistent approach for publicizing their work and results. Cutting edge research and articles of interest to a general public should be publicized through press releases (in much the same way that the *New England Journal of Medicine*, for instance, might publicize a new medical study). Given the "p.c." backlash and the mischaracterizations of women's studies in the media, it's essential that we create credible venues that get this information "out there" in clear, accessible language.

Yet the simple opposition between theory and accessibility also emerged as a deceptive one. Frances Shapiro-Skrobe and Donna Crawley, editors of *Transformations*, the New Jersey Project's journal devoted to curriculum transformation, wrote in response to my femedit request that:

> The overriding issue for us about editing a feminist journal is accessibility. Too often, language obscures content in feminist writing, particularly in writing that is highly "disciplinary." Jargon frightens people off from an article and it distances the reader from the author. Rather than working toward inclusiveness, the use of jargon excludes people from the "conversation." This is the issue that was threaded throughout the conference, linking to various speakers and sessions. It was gratifying and refreshing to hear renowned editors espouse the critical need for accessible writing and discuss the responsibility of editors to ensure that their journals are free of convoluted, self-serving, obfuscated language.
>
> Another aspect of accessibility explored at the conference was the fact that theory and accessible language are not mutually exclusive. Highly sophisticated ideas can and should be expressed simply. In fact, the more carefully thought out the idea, the more clearly it can be explained. We understand that not all readers have the background to read and understand all articles. However, our assumption is that the readers of feminist journals are, at the least, educated "lay" people who can follow the arguments presented in any article. Authors have a responsibility to write to this audience, while editors have a responsibility to provide a "common reader" as well as disciplinary readers to review a manuscript.

The need to be accessible is, of course, felt especially acutely by interdisciplinary journal editors. Others pointed out that theory itself has plural definitions and comes in several "languages."

Diana Strassmann, editor of a new journal, *Feminist Economics*, asked at one point what "theory" was for each of the editors and told us that, in mainstream economics, "theory" is set in opposition to "policy"—with theory envisaged as mathematical models; part of the mission of this new journal is to contest this formulation and to introduce alternative conceptualizations of "theory" more compatible with feminist thinking. In editing a social sciences journal, Sue Zalk produces copy that, she said, "is particularly inaccessible"—to readers from *within* as well as from without the social sciences: "there is no common language." I myself feel that language may require deliberate disruption if it is to move us to a more equitable place. But the conversations at this conference were testimony to an alternative practice of mutual recognition and cross-disciplinary dis-agreement, the variants among us traceable to our variant contexts, variant constituencies.

We returned again and again in the course of the conference to the practical-and-theoretical issue of "differences," and by difference, we meant never gender alone, but gender, class, race, ethnicity, and sexuality. The conference itself was, we all felt, too white. In the afternoon, in two roundtables on reviewing and manuscript selection—with Linda Gardiner, editor of *Women's Review of Books*, Barbara White, book review editor at *NWSA Journal*, Nancy Grey Osterud, editor of *Gender and History*, Linda Lopez McAlister, editor of *Hypatia*, and Claire Moses, managing editor of *Feminist Studies*—the practical problems of managing journals were foremost on the agenda. But the difficult struggle toward more equitable management and representation emerged, as it must, as the single most crucial issue for feminist editors.

Editors vary in how to develop a "multicultural" representation of authors, reviewers, and books reviewed, from the *Women's Review of Books'* intentionally "disproportionate" attention to works by and about marginalized women and groups—that is, their policy of looking longer and harder for and at such books, especially by and about African-American women rather than about whites—to *Gender and History's* international collective of editor/reviewers. In reply to my femedit request, Beverly Guy-Sheftall, founding co-editor of *SAGE: A Scholarly Journal on Black Women*, draws a sharp picture of how one journal became critical for women of color and especially for African-Americanists in the face of white feminists' indifference, their "erasures and gaps":

As founding co-editor of *SAGE: A Scholarly Journal on Black Women,* the first Black feminist publication of its kind, I have been immersed over the past decade in race/gender issues as they relate, in particular, to women of African descent locally and globally. Editing a journal focused on Black women has made me aware of the limitations of conventional feminist theory which has historically decentered or made invisible the activist, intellectual, and cultural work of a particular group of women who have been central to the development, nevertheless, of feminist criticism. In many ways *SAGE* emerged because of the failure of both Black Studies and Women's Studies to adequately address the experiences and thinking of Black women around the globe. Our editorial practice has been impacted in many ways, therefore, by the erasures and gaps in Black Studies and Women's Studies scholarship. For example, early on we published two issues on mother/daughter relationships in the Black community because the scholarship in the latter disciplines tended to ignore this important topic. We also published an issue on science/technology because of the scarcity of scholarship with respect to Black women in these areas as well. *SAGE* has been critical, we believe, to the development of Black Women's Studies and has helped in the reconceptualization of Women's Studies.

When *SAGE* was being conceptualized, we wanted to make sure that it was interdisciplinary, visually appealing, and accessible to a broad audience of women, especially Black women who were not necessarily consumers of scholarly publications. As editors we were committed to providing a publishing outlet for women of color, particularly Black women whose work may not have been appealing, for a number of reasons, to academic publications, including those focusing on women in general and Blacks. We were interested in publishing women who may not have published previously and who may have needed the kind of editorial assistance that very few well-established journals provide. We saw ourselves nurturing a new generation of scholars interested in Black Women's Studies and Black feminist scholarship. We were especially interested in broadening the definition of "scholarship" to include personal narratives which had an analytic framework.

Editing *SAGE* has made me more aware of the tremendous amount of scholarly work yet to be done on Black women in a variety of disciplines and on a number of topics. I am particularly aware of the scarcity of serious biographies on Black women and decided to do a biography on Anna Julia Cooper (1859-1964).

Editing *SAGE* has also taught me a great deal about the nature of collaborative work within a feminist framework. One of the disadvantages, however, of editing a feminist journal is that it is labor-intensive, under-staffed, and usually has limited resources. In other words, one makes do with less. A continuing challenge is establishing the kind of infrastructure which will sustain the journal over time. This work is truly a labor of love and sometimes interferes with one's own individual scholarship, perhaps the biggest drawback to a long-term commitment as editor.

SAGE remains as necessary as ever in the (otherwise) fast-changing world of scholarly journals. Capturing here the conflicting responsibilities of any feminist editor—echoing once more the worries of editors about accessibility, about mentorship, and about the basic practical hurdles and obligations of editing—and suffering herself from the risks of placing her knowledge and skill at the service of others' scholarship even when this means sacrificing time for her own, Beverly Guy-Sheftall nonetheless keeps centrally in view the motive force of her project, that is, to make room for women of color—to produce a genuinely collaborative feminism; and she recognizes her work as a labor of love.

Amidst the labor and the love, most feminist editors, nonetheless, find themselves occasionally wondering whether their efforts can have any lasting or wide effect. The day of the conference had begun with a friendly, but noisy debate about what feminist editors could, or should, do in the face of feminism's present-day obstacles and the conservative backlash (naturally enough, mass media—with its enormous reach and influence—became the focus of this discussion). In her opening remarks to the conference, Patsy Schweickart anticipated this discussion and suggested ways to think about our role. While she began by addressing the question of what it meant for feminist editors to meet simply to speak to each other, she moved from there to address the larger question of the role of a feminist editor within national and global feminist movements. The comments she sent me by femedit return to these remarks and extend them into a larger vision of what she persuasively describes as the dual purposes—and dual audiences—of feminist editing. We must address each other *and* others; we address worlds beyond journal audiences *and* ourselves. Circling back around to catch up the conference's beginnings in its possible ends, her commentary offers a final link to this report. I conclude, then, with her thoughts about who it is we should try to reach, why and how we can address both others and ourselves:

> At the conference, in my opening remarks, I said something about the idea of "preaching to the choir." I see my function as a feminist editor orchestrating this "preaching to the choir," or maybe, better, the choir preaching to each other.
> Very often, in feminist gatherings, one feels a sense of misgiving about those who are absent, and this sense of misgiving undermines our pleasure in those who are present in the gathering. The balance of regret and pleasure, of course, is a function of numbers—more regret/less pleasure the smaller the attendance. But even when the attendance is large, the theme of reaching out to those who are not present, who are not getting, are turned off by, are indifferent to our message—of

crafting the message to overcome barriers—of race, class, sexual orientation, age, nationality—tends to dominate our discourse and our reflections. As feminists, of course, we have to be concerned with persuading others, with recruiting more and more people to support the women's movement. I do not mean to underestimate the importance of this "missionary" function. But the feminist project has another dimension, which tends to be underestimated—that is, that of cultivating feminist culture, of appreciating, fostering and promoting the intellectual, emotional and moral qualities and the needs that emerged in us as a result of our engagement in feminism.

The problem can be posed another way: who is the addressee of feminist discourse? My answer is that we have a dual addressee—we address ourselves to the world at large (to all women and men of good will), and we address ourselves to each other, to the feminist community.

Feminist scholarship is a specific form of discourse whose principal aim is to foster the development of feminist studies—a branch of feminist culture. It is addressed principally to those who are conversant in feminist studies—in other words, to the converted. The principal addressees of *NWSAJ*, the journal I edit, are members of NWSA, and in general, teachers, scholars and students of the field of women's studies. In other words, the readership of the journal is constituted by people who are already converted to women's studies as a field of knowledge. The case is the same with any scholarly journal—for example, the readership of *PMLA* are principally those who work in the discipline of the modern languages; that of *Journal of Philosophy*, those in the discipline of philosophy. The reality of the discipline is accepted as a condition—as an enabling as well as constraining fact of life, even by those who engage in critical reflection about the discipline. The goal of the journal is to promote the development of the discipline.

If I were the editor of a scholarly journal in one of the "regular" disciplines—e.g. literature—I would not need to argue that the journal is addressed primarily to the experts in the field. But for a women's studies or feminist journal, there seems to be an essential irony—or contradiction—in addressing oneself principally to an academic elite. Our addressee, it seems, should be, at least, all women.

Why is it important to have a vehicle for this scholarly conversation? In what way does this scholarly conversation promote the feminist project? I have two answers, which are, in a sense, two sides of the same coin.

1. The realization of the feminist project requires the development of a publicly persuasive discourse—a discourse with some public authority. Academic discourse—the discourse of knowledge—is one component of such publicly persuasive discourse. The experiences and the perspectives of women have to be articulated in such a discourse. For example, women have long known about domestic violence and sexual harassment. They have known it in the sense that they have experienced it. They also have—as a result of this experience—knowledge of its psychology and its dynam-

ics; to some extent, how to protect oneself; how to avoid it; how to help victims. In other words, we had a knowledge in the form of "common sense." This knowledge, "common sense" was put to use by the first activists who established shelters. But in order to affect public policy, to revise laws, to get a share of public resources set aside for education, etc.—there was a need for research—publicly persuasive discourse—on domestic violence and sexual harassment. The currency of concepts such as "battered women's syndrome" and "sexual harassment" is the joint product of women's experience and common sense knowledge and feminist research.

2. The second reason has to do with the need to sustain a feminist culture—ourselves, the members of the choir, and a need to satisfy the intellectual and cultural energies that are awakened with the realization that women count, and women's perspectives count. In a sense, the feminist scholarship that is enabled by journals represents an anticipation of the fulfillment of the feminist project, a culture beyond male dominance, where women truly count, and where our reflections on what we are, and how life should be lived form a key part of the structures of knowledge.

Holly Laird, Associate Professor of English at the University of Tulsa, is editor of *Tulsa Studies in Women's Literature*. At present, she also holds the office of Vice President of the Council of Editors of Learned Journals. Her published work and teaching are engaged primarily with Victorian and modernist poetry and prose and with feminist theory, and she is currently at work on a feminist study of literary collaborations.

Cynthia Lucia

Working as an Editor at *Cineaste*

When writing and editing a publication about film, gender issues, by necessity, constitute a central concern. For the past three years, I have been one of six editors on the board of *Cineaste*, a quarterly publication devoted to the art and politics of the Hollywood, independent and international cinemas.

Writing and editing manuscripts which explore the representation of women in film continually poses the challenge of avoiding the simplistic and obvious conclusion that women are treated badly by Hollywood—more often than not, Hollywood films do exercise either an overt or subtle misogyny in their representation of women, particularly women in non-traditional roles. Beyond exposing such systems of representation, it is of paramount importance to identify the cultural/political conditions contributing to this misogny, both within individual films and in broader historical terms. While many mainstream publications often fall into the tempting trap of simply presenting the problem or of suggesting that the problem is well on its way to being solved through increased numbers of women working in the film industry, *Cineaste* has always questioned such broad assumptions and has encouraged in-depth analysis that honestly attempts to tackle the complex factors which shape the way women and other minority groups are represented in film.

Although a leftist publication, *Cineaste* strives to avoid the clichés of the left and single-note political takes on film issues which may obscure rather than uncover the workings of *competing* ideologies. This goal, though we may not always accomplish it as fully as we wish, applies to issues of feminist concern, as well as to other significant political and aesthetic concerns, such as those involving gay and lesbian representations, race and ethnicity in film, and third world cinema, to name a few.

As the only female board member, I am frequently looked upon as the "expert" on feminist issues or the spokesperson for various feminist film criticism projects submitted to the magazine. I'm not entirely comfortable with that position, partially because I'm not sure I can claim greater expertise, by simple virtue of being female, than that of the male board members, who are feminists to varying degrees. Recent trends encourage us to look for expert critics on the representational politics of marginal groups only among members of those groups. While this practice offers much-deserved and long overdue credibility to voices that traditionally have been silenced or largely ignored, it does, to some extent, limit the texture and various angles of debate on feminist or other minority political issues.

Economics certainly plays a large part in the minority status most of us hold on editorial boards and, in this case, in my single voice being granted a privileged position in respect to feminist film issues. Although women have been a part of the *Cineaste* board since the mid-70s, they have always constituted a minority in an organization dominated by men. While the magazine has made aggressive efforts to recruit additional female members as associates, with the goal of eventually asking those women to assume positions as editors, the fact that *Cineaste* is an entirely voluntary commitment has discouraged women and other minority members who cannot devote hours of their time to non-paying work. Many women *Cineaste* has approached, because of inequities in pay and job opportunities, are often less secure in their earning power than men and, therefore, less available to work for no pay. And because child care continues to fall primarily upon female shoulders, talented professional women have even less time to devote to an all-volunteer endeavor such as *Cineaste*, which requires weekly office work in New York City, hours of writing and editorial work, as well as monthly weekend meetings. Likewise, the number of other minority groups able to volunteer time is severely limited by economic conditions which seem to dictate that few minorities enter film or film-related fields in college, severely limiting staffing diversity on a publication such as *Cineaste*.

In writing and editing manuscripts from a feminist perspective, I firmly adopt the magazine's position that such writing should be accessible to a broad, though admittedly educated audience. Because feminist film theory, in particular, is jargon-laden and circuitous, it often limits itself to a very narrow audience of academics. In accepting manuscripts and working with writers, the *Cineaste* editors attempt to make feminist film criticism clear and accessible, without diluting its content. Striking the balance between accessibility and depth is especially challenging when academic language does reflect layered concepts and thinking. Too often, however, jargon attempts to camouflage prose lacking in true theoretical substance and/or in concrete value to its readers. Primarily, we, as feminist writers and editors, have a moral obligation to communicate our ideas clearly to as broad a readership as possible; otherwise we emulate the same exclusionary power games men have traditionally played.

Working as an editor at *Cineaste* has deeply influenced my work as a teacher of high school English and film, as I'm sure most of us have found other areas of our lives influenced by our work in a field dominated by men. On a daily basis, I witness the subtle erosion of confidence and self-assurance teenage girls experience, as boys seem to grow ever more assertive and self-assured. Encouraging these young women to find their own voices as writers and to speak within a classroom environment in which other teenage girls and boys will truly listen—in an environment where the female voice carries authority and commands respect—will, hopefully, enable these girls to fight effectively against the economic and cultural barriers they very likely will face as they move on to college and the working world.

As with many of us, my editorial work at *Cineaste* has, without a doubt, deepened my commitment to feminist principles, yet it has deepened my recognition of how far we have yet to travel before large numbers of women and other minorities truly are provided with the economic foundation to pursue the multiplicity of opportunities that have been more readily available to men.

Jennifer Moxley

That with this bright believing band
I have no claim to be,
That faiths by which my comrades stand
Seem fantasies to me . . .

—from "The Impercipient"

"The Impercipient" is a Thomas Hardy poem after which I named my small magazine. I say "mine" for I started the magazine on my own and I am the sole editor. Friends chip in for proofing and stapling when I'm in a bind but other than that I am in charge of every other aspect relating to the magazine. While production is never an independent venture (I need the Xerox and postal workers, the paper makers, printers, and of course, the poets), editorship of *The Impercipient* is non-collaborative, and to have it be so was a completely conscious decision.

Originally my lover (who is male) and I had planned to start up a journal together. We thought it sounded like a fun project, more fun than trying to break into the already defined spaces of the journals we read. Everything out there seemed so impacted (like a bum tooth), for any poetry journal (including *The Impercipient*) you follow long enough will eventually exhibit a coterie of favorites and into this small band of bright believers new friends are let in a few at a time providing they conform to an already articulated journal image. "Conform" is certainly too strong a word, for the journals we read in part determine our aesthetic choices, and so naturally like young recruits if we hang on long enough promotion is almost certain. Sometimes conformism is in order, other times dissent and irreverence are the winning cards to play. This is the "I like your spunk" school of editorial power, and falsely assumes an "open-mindedness" to "true" talent, even when it goes against previous editorial patterns. Of course, depending on the day, I am not all that bitter about publishing, and starting a magazine was actually an adventure begun more amorphously than not. And then my lover . . . well we haggled over every aspect of how to proceed and the final break came over naming the magazine. I realized that our collaboration wasn't going to work. We dropped the idea and went on with our other commitments, including the one to each other. Then about a year later I announced that I was going to start a magazine, I didn't even

ask if he wanted to be a part of it. I rejected one of those asi-
nine kindergarten maxims and "did not share." There were a
few hurt/guilt days to follow but it wasn't long before he
accepted my decision as if it were his own.

My lover and I have different work methods but similar aesthetics and virtually identical values. I believe collaborating on
the magazine failed because firstly he's a man and I'm a woman,
and secondly because he's a Ph.D. candidate and I was at the
time working on finishing my ten-year long B.A. And so while
power is fun in some rooms, I knew if we collaborated on *The
Impercipient*, I (who am no wallflower) would have become
intimidated by his presence and judgment and before long
would have started to turn to him for approval on every decision I made. Not because I think he is smarter than me, or even
because he thinks he is smarter than me, but because the world
we live in thinks so and I cannot always fight the insecurity and
frustration that necessarily results from this fact. However to
fully understand my predicament and subsequent choices to
edit alone we must go beyond Hardy's lines "That with this
bright believing band / I have no claim to be." The following
lines of the poem are "That faiths by which my comrades stand
/ seem fantasies to me." (Hardy is referring to the Christian
faith but I can extrapolate and reconstruct the argument for
modern day acolytes.) You see the problem with my lover is
not that he is male, it's that the world notices he is male, and
believes his outfit, while less stylish, is more serious than mine.
The world also sees that he is becoming professionalized and
therefore grants him more validity than me, *from the get go*. I
have to "win" (a dubious word) authority (another dubious
word), his comes with the outfit, which also has its disadvantages, but too few I think to note here. Extending yet continuing Hardy's idiom I call this strange phenomenon "Gender
Faith." And like other faiths there exists no real evidence to
substantiate it, only a long standing system of belief with which
to explain everything from the unknowable to the unthinkable.
Hardy's "I have no claim to be" might be misinterpreted as a
submissive gesture of humbleness, but it is not. After all, you
have to at least believe you own the coat before turning in your
claim check, and Hardy denies any evidence that would lead
him to this belief. The *disbelief* he feels comes from his perception that the *belief* of others is founded on "fantasies."

I chose to step aside, both from a male/female collaboration
and from acceptance into established journals, not because I
dismiss these battles as impossible or unworthy to fight (otherwise I wouldn't be living with this guy) but because I had and

continue to have confidence in my own vision. It is a vision founded on impercipience, or if you will, on disbelief. And like the lines from the third stanza of Hardy's poem, this disbelief is not a desire but a discomfort: "Since heart of mind knows not that ease / Which they know; since it be / That He who breathes All's-Well to these / Breathes no All's-Well to me." I do not perceive the value of much that goes on in the world, even in the wonderful world of poetry. I am privileged enough to have the means and leisure to produce an alternate, dissenting opinion, and so I do. But I am not addicted to dissent, or to fighting for each straw of recognition when I do not have to. I decided to do the magazine alone precisely because it gave me a space in which I did not have to fight. I do not practice monogamy nor advocate separatism in love or poetry, but I think that exclusion and retreat can sometimes be strategically advantageous. I can benefit from withdrawing because I am educated and live in a democracy (though it's often nominal). Gender inequality affects me every time I feel unsafe in my country, but for the most part, because of my class position, it's a home front battle. I am conscious but not crippled by the immunity I have to discover forgotten resources and build strength, which allows me the time to construct the best form of counter-attack. And here is where Hardy and I part ways, for he ends, "The Impercipient": "Enough. As yet disquiet clings / About us. Rest shall we." Whereas I advocate not ending with rest but rather with agitation. And so perhaps in my case the word "magazine" refers to its other definition, that is, a storehouse of ammunition.

Susan Smith Nash

On Editing And Publishing A Small Magazine: Saddle-Stitching Away From The Margin

It is tempting to think that the task of editor of a literary journal is one of evaluating, sorting, and selecting, and not one of writing. However, if one begins to think of editing in terms of interactions with and management of discourse, then it's not too great a leap to think of editing and writing as essentially the same enterprise. Because editing produces a large text (the journal) from smaller ones (the pieces), one endpoint of editing is the creation of a new entity—a piece of discourse that possesses an individuated body, its own morphology, and even a level of autonomy.

Simply stated, one goal of editing is to construct a new thing (the journal) from old things. As such, editing constitutes metamorphosis. This is a directed metamorphosis, however, since a function of editing is also discourse production, as is writing. Yet, often the artist or author is considered the "creator" while the editor is given a more lowly position—that of barber or manicurist, an almost parasitic presence whose only function is to present the works of art in their best light.

As editor and publisher I've come to value the process of assembling and publishing texts. I think of my task as one of managing form, and that my primary task is a rhetorical (or persuasive) one. However, I think that other forms are represented as well—including the categories of discourse that James L. Kinneavy refers to in *A Theory of Discourse*. The forms of discourse represented in the magazine which I edit and publish, *texture*, include informational, expressive, and heuristic (or exploratory) which Kinneavy refers to as scientific.

In assembling texts in order to persuade an audience of their validity, I have developed a few strategies. First and foremost, I try to position *texture* so that it can join in the contemporary conversation on poetics. Somewhere in the dialogue, I'd like *texture*'s voice to both engage and cohere with those who merge author, critic, and publisher roles. This desire requires an endorsement of the ideological position that poets should develop self-awareness or self-consciousness of their own writing procedures and that they acquire a good grounding in theory. I want *texture*'s readers to understand this experience as a coming together of poetry and poetics. Specifically, I am interested in experimental (including but not limited to Language-centered) poetry and the accompanying criticism and theory. By foregrounding both, the magazine is both a construction and its own reality; therefore, *texture* constitutes a reification of a poetics of experimentation.

By integrating poetry and poetic theory, the constructed discourse (*texture*) tends to function as a validating, legitimizing agent which exists, in part, to correct prevailing views that poetry and theory must be separate, and that the poem privileges empirical systems of knowledge. Given this stance, *texture* maintains that the artist or writer can reposition and recast poetic conventions. Instead of constructing a poem that relies on the reader's familiarity with what the culture considers to be shared (even universal) sensations and motivations (in the terms of Adam Smith's writings on "common sense" and the entire Scottish Enlightenment's stance on this issue), the poet can write a poem that plays with language in order to explore and exploit the refractory quality of language. There are limitless possibilities embodied in this rhetorical strategy, since such a poetic stance can foreground, question, and play with the audience's fluency in the dominant culture's icons.

I don't want to imply that I have a dogmatic and rigid ideological agenda that overarches and constrains *texture* and the other Texture Press publications—the chapbooks, miniatures, and the occasional newsletter, *exposures*. While I do consciously seek to persuade my audience, I have to admit that my audience, for the most part, has already been persuaded of the notions I have articulated here. They bring to the reading an already-encoded stance that corresponds with those who seek to reposition writing that has been marginalized or ignored. There is an irony here, of course, because in order to "reposition" something, I must believe in the model of reality that maintains that there is, as Cornel West puts it, a cultural politics of difference. To acknowledge this model does some damage. I have to speculate where *texture* might be in relation to the "margin" and the "center"—the result of such analysis could be quite discouraging, even alienating.

Feminist theory has helped me a great deal by giving me a vocabulary of "influence-rearrangement" (I prefer this catchphrase to ones that rely on the word, "power"; that word is too reductive). I often think of what Audre Lorde wrote in her essay, "Age, Race, Class, and Sex: Women Redefining Difference" which appears in *Out There: Marginalization and*

Contemporary Cultures, a collection of essays edited by Russell Ferguson, Martha Gever, Trinh T. Minh-ha and Cornel West (New York: New Museum of Contemporary Art, 1990):

> For we have, built into all of us, old blueprints of expectation and response, old structures of oppression, and these must be altered at the same time as we alter the living conditions which are a result of those structures (Lorde 287).

I think this applies to a literary magazine as well as to the culture as a whole. We can be trapped by internalized expectations of what a literary magazine is, what it looks like, how it presents the material, etc.—but we have to try to break free of the grip of expectations. Otherwise, we will unconsciously perpetuate old structures of discourse. The structures can be oppressive—but I would like to suggest that the old structures aren't always oppressive. We need to alter them anyway in order to provide more options for ourselves as we go through life constructing our own scripts and texts.

I'd love to have a limitless budget to put together an entire catalogue of gorgeous books. However, I am constrained by money. Although *texture* has subscribers and is carried by a few bookstores and distributors, it doesn't break even. I foot the bill. As a result, I've developed the mindset, "small is beautiful, cheap is good" which I repeat mantra-like to myself in order to not disappoint myself as I compare my press's publications with the expectations I have already encoded within my consciousness. Nevertheless, issues of design are extremely important to me, primarily because I am interested in all manifestations of *logos*. I have published visual poetry, photography, and art, and I would be interested in publishing a graphic short story (in the tradition of Art Spiegelman's *Maus*, but in black and white) or graphic poems.

I'm planning to continue to publish *texture* as long as I can. It has been an emotionally rewarding experience, and I have felt connected with other people who share similar interests. Of course, I have to be careful not to burn myself out, because, as I'm sure all editors will say, editing and publishing can be grueling, demanding work. Not only does one have to assemble the texts, one has to typeset, proof, do the layout, negotiate with printers, and distribute the magazine. In the midst of this is the issue of correspondence, which does take time. Despite all the work and expense involved, I still have the nerve to encourage people to start a magazine or pamphlet series. I am firmly convinced that the energy and diversity of the small press (or micropress) scene is absolutely essential to the development of art in America. If our government won't fund us, we have to do it ourselves—small is beautiful, cheap is good!

Texture Press began in 1989 with the publication of a series of broadsides which feature experimental poetics juxtaposed with art or photographs. From the beginning, the focus has centered around a "revisioning gaze"—that is to say that I'm interested in *inventio* and the constructivist view that texts do more than represent the world, they actually recast and recreate it. In 1990, *texture* magazine was launched. It was a modest affair of only 4 pages. Since then, it has expanded, and *texture* #5 contains 64 pages, 8 1/2 x 11, perfect bound, with work from Juliana Spahr, Clark Coolidge, Ray DiPalma, Beth Joselow, Laura Feldman, Ed Foster, Liz Brennan, and others. In addition to the magazine, there is a chapbook series. At this point there are 12 books in the series, and authors include Heather Thomas, Valerie Fox, Rochelle Owens, and Cydney Chadwick. *Texture* is indexed in the American Humanities Index. The magazine and chapbooks are distributed in the U.S. by Anton Mikofsky, and are available at several university libraries and bookstores throughout the U.S. Texture Press publications are also distributed by Spectacular Diseases (England), Julien Blaine (France), and Vattacharja Chandan (India).

Marjorie Perloff

1) How has editing influenced your other work?
My experiences have ranged from excellent to awful. Awful for the *Columbia Literary History*. I thought when I took on this task that I could put my own stamp on the way we look at the contemporary literary/cultural scene. I especially wanted to introduce readers to the more radical poetries and fictions and downplay John Updike and Joyce Carol Oates, etc. It turned out that the volume's editor insisted on certain contributors and certain coverage. The book ended up having three chapters on contemporary fiction (because it was thought that Raymond Federman's delightfully iconoclastic chapter on metafiction versus the Old Realism was too unkind to the mainstream) and only one on poetry! The issue of inclusion, coverage, and a mechanical diversity, constantly came up and, as a result, the final product has very little to do with me. Yet it was very time-consuming. Still, I'm pleased when I travel and hear, as I just did at the University of Salzburg in Austria, that Henry Sayre's chapter on experimental writing has been read and enjoyed by the local faculty and students.

At the other extreme, editing *Postmodern Genres* and *John Cage: Composed in America* was a joy because I chose all the contributors, chose only those I knew I could count on, and the results seem very fine to me. For the John Cage book, I've had the experience of having a wonderful co-editor, Charles Junkerman, who did a lot of the leg work and who had organized the original conference on which the book was based. So it was a pleasure and we both learned a lot.

3) Editing as power or subversion of it:
Well, I do feel editing takes precious time away from one's own writing. It's a chore, a secondary role, and I always want to be doing my own thing. In this sense it's a subversion of power. On the other hand, there are brilliant editors like Jerome Rothenberg whose choice of materials and coordination thereof are important artistic and cultural documents in their own right. Editing an anthology can be extremely rewarding, allowing one to determine what will and what won't be read by a large number of readers.

6, 7, 8) Academic publications now tend to publish almost as many women as men; it's no longer a major issue in this sense.

Still, there are insidious problems. Men (male editors) are delighted to receive feminist essays, especially ones that foreground feminist theory. But if you're a woman who happens not to want to foreground that theory, watch out. Because that's your slot and they're not too eager to put you in their slot. At this writing, *New Literary History* is sitting on my desk. The topic for the Autumn 1993 issue is Literary and Cultural Change. The contributors are 11 men and two women, Helene Cixous and Mary Carruthers (a medievalist). Are women, then, not interested in Cultural Change? Cixous's piece is on Bathsheba, a personal and lyrical meditation on Rembrandt's well-known portrait. All the "serious" pieces in the journal on "Higher Education in the 1990s" (Geoffrey Hartman), "Deconstruction as Second-Order Observing" (Niklas Luhmann), "Environment, Environmentalists, and Global Change" (Reid A. Bryson)—are by men. So both in the John Cage book and in *Postmodern Genres*, I tried to be sure to have as many women contributors (e.g., Joan Retallack, Katharine Hayles, Jann Pasler, Linda Hutcheon, Jessica Prinz, Renee Hubert) as men but not to place them in the "subaltern" slot.

How do women fit into the exchange economy of editorial practice? They have made real inroads in poetry/poetics magazines (e.g. Lyn Hejinian's editing of *Poetics Journal* or Cydney Chadwick's *Avec*) but less in the academy, except in the case of the exclusively "women's journals" like *Signs* and *Tulsa Studies in Women's Literature*. The editors of the most prestigious journals like *Critical Inquiry*, *New Literary History*, *Common Knowledge*, *American Literary History* still tend to be men. In this exchange economy, women assume lesser roles and of course they staff the offices. But there are signs that this is now changing. *October* is an example of a women-run journal and certainly it's among the most interesting journals around. Still, Rosalind Krauss and Annette Michelson have evidently gotten a lot of flack, even from their own board, and that doesn't happen too often in the case of journals edited by men.

Marjorie Perloff has edited a special number of *Contemporary Poetry* on Modern British Poetry and *Postmodern Genres* (U of Oklahoma Press, 1989), as well as the contemporary literature section of the *Columbia Literary History of the U.S.* Forthcoming is *John Cage: Composed in America* from the University of Chicago Press in 1994.

Rena Rosenwasser

Chain/Kelsey St. Press

Writing constantly refers to writing and no writing can be free of other writings.
> —Trinh T. Minh-ha, *HOW(ever)*, V:4

When we, the six founders of Kelsey St. Press, began as publishers we were aware of the authorial presence of the female voice in literature. The actuality of Woolf, Stein, and H.D. resonated in readings that we read to ourselves and to each other. We were going back to sources, conscious of how these writers had been neglected in our own college studies. The textual sound of Adrienne Rich reading *Diving Into The Wreck* had just occurred. We were women, five of us poets, who had been meeting in a group to read and provide critical commentary on each other's work. It was nineteen-seventy-three.

What I call the cultural field of language is made of male sexual and psychic energies transformed through centuries of written fiction into standards for imagination, frames of references, patterns of analysis, networks of meaning, rhetorics of body and soul.
> —Nicole Brossard, "Poetic Politics,"
> *The Politics of Poetic Form*

When we began the press, we were also incensed by the absence of female authority in the books we saw around us. An anthology of Bay Area Beat Poets had just been released. It neglected to mention women writers. We bitterly resented this deletion in a history that canonized the Beat poetic voice. Co-founding a press to publish new writing by women was a means of questioning the centrality of the male figure in writing. It was nineteen seventy-four.

And if we consult literary history, it is the same story. It all comes back to man—to this torment, his desire to be (at) the origin.
> —Helene Cixous and Catherine Clement,
> "Sorties," *The Newly Born Woman*

We wished to make editorial decisions that would give the writing by women we valued a *place*. We saw the book, the art of letterpress bookmaking, as a way of allocating a form that could *not* be easily put aside. A well-made book was an object that would hold sufficient tension. We wanted the new writing by women to actually have physical weight that we, with the help of hard metal type and the roller's force, would impart to their words. In printing, finding the perfect pressure was a goal that craft would hone. I learned to hand-set letterpress type. Patricia Dienstfrey worked on an old Vandercook Press. It took time. We were slow. But our hands locked the metal type into the press's bed, pushed the rollers over the type until the desired impression was exacted on the paper. In San Francisco, during this period, many other women were learning techniques of fine printing. One could easily view this period as a renaissance of the craft of printing. The old fine printing traditions of the Grabhorn Press were being revived. This time women printers were at the hub of this activity. Few of the presses begun then have survived. Today many of these women attend to their art by teaching letterpress printing in college bookmaking programs. They are training a younger generation, many of whom are women writers and artists, in their passion for the book arts. Kathy Walkup, Frances Butler, Jaime Robles are among these exceptionally fine printers. Printing wasn't writing and we were all writers, but it was close to writing. We found the proper balance, after the type was locked up in the bed, between too little and too much pressure.

Kelsey St. Press's actual imprint was made, in Berkeley, on our first release, a translation of the Italian poet, Margherita Guidacci's *Neurosuite*. Marina La Palma, one of the original founders, translated the work. When we finished collating and hand-stitching the book it was nineteen-seventy-five.

> *A strange dialectic is set up in which going beyond is brought about by the actual gap between a lost past and a future that rediscovers it.*
>
> —Cixous and Clement, "The Guilty One,"
> *The Newly Born Woman*

The seventies passed with all its feminist concerns mapped in the books we made and how we made them. Pat and I continued to print some of our poetry books on letterpress, while other press members produced poetry and short fiction on offset. As other activities made demands on our time, our ability to actually make, print the works on the Vandercook press diminished. The other business of running a press began to gain precedence. We were besieged with manuscripts; we were constantly raising money by writing grants and fund-raising from a local community of supportive women. The original group of Pat, Marina and myself, as well as Karen Brodine, Laura Moriarty and Kit Duane changed over the next decade and a half. Pat and I remained. With the end of the seventies, many revisions and reversions had altered our perceptions of what the book was that we wanted to make (publish).

> *. . . uneasiness—dissatisfaction with existing forms may result in the formal integration of these doubts by the creation of new forms, forms that in one way or another exceed or surpass our expectations.*
> —Lydia Davis, *HOW(ever)*, IV:2

Our reading and writing, as editors and as poets, kept challenging our notions of content and form. If there was a boundary we recognized, we looked for work that took on that boundary. In the eighties the practices of women poets that we came into contact with asserted itself by taking on formal issues. No longer was the focus simply the content of gendered experience. Language itself, the rubrics of syntax, grammar, the actual lexicon became the subject. We were passionately reading Irigaray, Cixous, Kristeva and the French Canadian "écriture au feminine" movement. Gender obviously addressed issues of what content was, but the less obvious and ultimately more revolutionary practice was to take on literary form and turn it inside out.

> *And what about the women poets who were writing experimentally? Oh, were there women poets writing experimentally . . . Yes there were . . .*
> *And the women poets, the ones you call experimentalist, were they reading Simone de Beauvoir? Firestone? Chodorow? Irigaray? Some were. They were reading and they were thinking backwards and forwards. They were writing to re-imagine how the language might describe the life of a woman thinking and changing. And the poetry they were writing wasn't fitting into anybody's anything because there wasn't a clear place made for it.*
> —Kathleen Fraser, *HOW(ever)*, I:1

How(ever) magazine, formed by Kathleen Fraser, Frances Jaffer, and Beverly Dahlen was a marker. The Bay Area, with this critical literary journal, had once more positioned itself as a locale where new practices, readings and rereadings could converge. This time the nexus would be experimental writing by women.

Kelsey St. Press was deeply involved and engaged with the makers and writers and ideas crossing these pages. This momentum catapulted our editorial concerns forward. It was nineteen-eighty-three.

> *Poetics is derived from philosophical and structuralist studies of literature descriptive of the way sounds, words and sentences form literary units.*
> —Erica Hunt, "Notes for an Oppositional Poetics,"
> *The Politics of Poetic Form*

Our editorial commitments were pushed out in all directions by this confluence of ideas and stimuli. We were moving more and more, in our choice of what writing we would publish, to work that took risks in breaking traditional linguistic frames. At the same time, we were interested in issues of identity, and were looking for women writers who were approaching these ideas in fresh and challenging ways.

> *Does "the feminine" resist representation within language . . . Where and how do compulsory heterosexuality and phallogocentrism converge? . . . How does language itself produce the fictive construction of "sex" that supports these various regimes of power? . . . What kinds of cultural practices produce subversive discontinuity and dissonance among sex gender and desire and call into question their alleged relations?*
> —Judith Butler, *Gender Trouble*

Pat and I had been reading and discussing theory all along. Our writing and editorial concerns kept making quantum leaps. As a lesbian, I was interested in texts that took task with sexuality and gender construction. Queer theory, theater, performance art, and fine art that spoke to these issues preoccupied me. In my own writing practices and as an editor I felt stimulated by these shifting positions.

> *You cannot foresee if the words arousing her are vulgar ancient or foreign or if it is the whole sentence that attracts her and quickens in her a desire like a scent of the embrace a way of feeling her body as truly ready for everything. Nothing is foreseen Yet the mouth of bodies commoving aroused by the words by instinct finds the image that arouses.*
> —Nicole Brossard, *Sous La Langue (Under Tongue)*,
> translated by Suzanne de Lotbinière-Harwood

By the late eighties Kelsey St. Press's attention to bookmaking was re-addressed by initiating a series of collaborations between poets and visual artists. The notion of the solitary artist constructing a body of work with the authority of a single ego at its core would be subverted. Invite two women, a poet and a visual artist, to interfere with each other's personal space of authorship. Each would let go of the privacy of her process, and in turn her ego authority over the primacy of that process. They would submit to each other's questions and responses. On the level of language, subject and object are more at risk. On the level of image, an image might emerge that never would have crossed the artist's mind. Embarking on this collaborative series was a way of scrutinizing ideas concerning the unity of identity (the unity of the subject). How much risk might be taken in the effort to disrupt the way an individual constructs herself through her art? The book would emerge as an artwork that accumulated at the nexus of these cross-hatched authorities.

My passion for painting and poetry was inflamed by the book-making potentials inherent in this negotiation. Collaboration challenged western history's insistence on the artist as male pro-genitor, the genius forging forward on *his* own. Collaboration between two women would further break down the traditional constructions of the solitary "artiste." The actual production of these books would also challenge the bookmaker in me. How to produce, using off-set printing, some of the feeling of the "livres des peintres," but also keep the cost down? We had begun the press with the conviction that the books we publish should be affordable to poets. At the same time I wanted to make the book itself a breathing vehicle for new forms. I was instrumental in initiating this new Kelsey St. Press series. My brother Robert Rosenwasser, who is an artist and designer, was hired by the press to work with me and the artists on our collaborations. He and I work well together; our visual aesthetic aligns. Making collaborations work has been an extreme source of pleasure to me as poet, bookmaker and lover of painting.

> But we are not only women living at the end of the twentieth century, but also women who—thanks to the struggles of the last twenty years—are hearing ourselves better, more profoundly than ever before . . . Still the process of knowing the written word into some new shape better suited to our use goes on it seems with

increasing insistence. A community is being formed, cutting across cultures and resistances.

—Gail Scott, *HOW(ever)*, VI: 4

This year, Kelsey St. Press celebrates its twentieth anniversary. We have a full production schedule planned. The poetry and prose works we are about to do claim new identity and linguistic positions. The range and quality of manuscripts we receive is stirring. Challenging writing is submitted to us by more authors than at any time in our long life. This is either a statement about the creative level in the community of experimental writers or a reflection of the literary community's perception of our role as a women's press devoted to innovative writing. Both probably bear some validity. Denise Liddell Lawson (a recent press member), Patricia Dienstfrey and myself, as editors, are more excited than ever about the prospects of poetic practices in the coming years. We have no desire to increase the volume of books we produce each year but, rather, to continue pushing the boundaries of the books we do make. It is nineteen ninety-four.

Rena Rosenwasser is the director of Kelsey St. Press

Phyllis Rosenzweig

Primary Writing has been devoted to one longish work by one writer per issue. In producing it I suppose I conflated the roles of publisher/editor because once I asked someone for work I edited only in the sense of checking for typos, etc. I am not sure what you mean by other work. I don't think editing (or publishing) influences my other writing but it does clarify (rather than influence) aspects of what I like about my "day job," which has to do with facilitating the public presentation of other people's work. But I purposely kept the production of *Primary Writing* very low tech so that I could be "the boss" and retain control of it. In that sense questions about gender and power are mixed in my mind. I am incredibly generous and malleable as long as things get done (pretty much) my way. Is that feminine or masculine? I *do* like working *with* women. I am also very possessive. I think my primary obligation as an editor/publisher is to my writers. (*My* writers). Thus I owe attention to design and production (which I like) and the tedium of distribution (which I hate) to them but I have the hubris to think that I shine in their reflected brilliance. The collective positive power of women is very thrilling to me and I like the idea of a publication defined by gender (although there are a few exceptional men I am sure I would want to include from time to time). I'm not sure what to say about academic publications, especially if you mean literary criticism, because I am somewhat out of that loop. The amount of literature in art history, my "legitimate" profession, is enormous. Much of it remains devoted to the study of the individual male geniuses who make up the heretofore linear history of western art, and a great deal of it has been written complicitly by women (Patriarchy is an equal opportunity employer?). On the other hand the liveliest writing in the professional journals takes into account questions of overt vs. covert subject matter, audience and patronage. I think of this as a feminist method of deconstruction, pioneered in consciousness raising groups in the early 1970s, although much of it has been coopted by male writers. This has been a lengthy digression. Feminist theory has certainly influenced my own publication practice—beginning with the very fact of conceiving the possibility of publishing my own journal—if by osmosis rather than specific example. I find the questions of economy and aesthetic practices as difficult to separate as those of power and gender, but the *Chain* project seems to embody the exploration of them all. It is very exciting.

Three issues of *Primary Writing* exist so far, having come out one per year: "Via Negativa" by Jane DeLynn in 1983, 21 pp., $3.00; "Scale Sliding (The Ambiguous Figures Project)" by Tina Darragh in 1984, 18 pp., $4.00 [to cover re-printing]; "Three Novels" by Doug Lang in 1985, 18 pp., $3.00. Forthcoming: "Doug Lang/Phyllis Rosenzweig/Diane Ward/Reading at the Corcoran." All newsletter format, corner stapled. Available from Phyllis Rosenzweig, 2009 Belmont Rd. NW #203, Washington DC 20009. Although produced casually, and for my own pleasure, the publication rate has been a lot more sporadic than I originally intended, and I resist putting it in the past tense because I always still intend to put out another issue. Publishing it has been one of the most satisfying experiences in my life.

Mira Schor

I became an editor within a couple of years of beginning to write about art; in a very real sense I learned on the job how to edit. My teachers were *my* editors. On the one hand Susan Bee's interventions into my writings have always served to clarify my text, eliminate personal digressions and inappropriate confessions, and generally get me out of trouble! On the other hand, I have occasionally contended with more intrusive editors . . . in one case almost every sentence had been rewritten and journalistic snap phrases added by one such a well-meaning but invasive editor although, in a marathon session, I eventually won back almost all of my language. Between these poles of fairness and interference, I learned for myself as a writer and as an editor how to look at a text for what needs to be said in the clearest, cleanest prose possible without altering the style and spirit of the writer. I enjoy editing, I enjoy getting out a red pencil and digging in! Susan Bee and I are compatible as editors because we have a basic agreement on what makes a readable text, and she is an excellent copy editor, stitching nimbly through the text picking out unnecessary words and silly ideas, while I think I'm good at broad restructuring. Despite my experiences with overbearing editors, I act without ambivalence on my feelings about a text's form and concept.

I've enjoyed the very small but real power of being the proprietor of a space for ideas, I've enjoyed the pathetically meager perks of being an editor, such as receiving review copies of books. The sense of community with our loyal subscribers makes up for the hours of unpaid labor. But editing *M/E/A/N/I/N/G* is only one of several activities—I am primarily a painter, I teach to make a living, I lecture, and I also write—and I think it is a healthy thing that I can only give the texts submitted to *M/E/A/N/I/N/G* relatively little time and focus. I work with the writer and on the text just enough to get it in shape. Then I am reabsorbed by my other responsibilities. I think this is true for Susan as well, and I suspect that the part-time nature of our editorial practice combined with our full-time identities as working artists has dispersed our roles as potential power brokers and given us a light and open touch as editors, relative to fulltime professionals in the field.

I began to write and became an editor at the same time that I began to paint in oil on canvas and linen after years of working with pastel, dry pigment, and gouache on paper. These earlier media did not allow much change from one's first action. I generally finished a piece in a day or two. However text can, usually must be changed—I was at first amazed to find that, after a couple of days or weeks, the areas that needed pruning or clarifying sprang off the page so that the act of rewriting did not feel like a violent transgression of my work but a welcome necessity. Similarly, as a technical characteristic, oil allows for endless transformation. This trait of text interacted synergistically with the mutability of oil painting. Each process gave me courage to be more ruthless with my original idea in either practice.

I think *M/E/A/N/I/N/G* has been defined by the gender *and the feminism* of its editors, but also by our desire to create an undogmatic space, to address aesthetics as well as politics, to allow men to address gender and other issues. *M/E/A/N/I/N/G* was created as a point of intersection between the critical theory so prevalent in mid-80s art writing and visual art practice. Postmodernist and "French Feminist" theories often were presented in highly dogmatic and exclusionary forms in other journals of contemporary art and culture. While my writing was informed by these discourses, it has been particularly important to me to create a space for more open dialogue because of my earlier experiences with organized feminism. I was a participant in the Feminist Art Program at CalArts in 1971 which I always refer to as boot camp for feminists because it had many of the faults of any program of radical and separatist indoctrination, while also being a rare occasion for highly focused feminist leadership training. I emerged suspicious of dogmatism and leery of large groups. *M/E/A/N/I/N/G* has been an ideal situation for me: two women of similar background but with different personalities, with loosely shared but sometimes wildly differing feminist and aesthetic viewpoints, making all the decisions quickly, without having to adhere to a party line or to wait for twenty other women to make up their minds (I've heard enough about the trials and tribulations of producing *Heresies*, a journal of feminist collectives, to know it would have driven me insane to work in that system!). Our experience with *M/E/A/N/I/N/G* leads me to trust in the political efficacy of small cells. I recommend small publications as a feminist arena and strategy.

Mira Schor edits *M/E/A/N/I/N/G* with Susan Bee. See description of journal following Bee's statement.

Meredith Stricker

Everyday's an experiment in livelihood: working outside an institutional center. How to stay alive in unauthorized, freely moving language? Speaking to & with each other. Somehow—invent without ending. *HOW(ever)* appearing now for eight years against a much greater likelihood of "blank pages": the unprinted & uncirculated—leaves something in motion, like the images H.D. reads: *"inevitably a shadow, a writing-on-the-wall, a curve like a reversed, unfinished S and a dot beneath it, a question mark, the shadow of a question . . ."*
—*Meredith Stricker*

from <u>HOW(ever)</u> *Vol. VI, No. 4*

a munkához, a hosszas helyettesítéskes. t

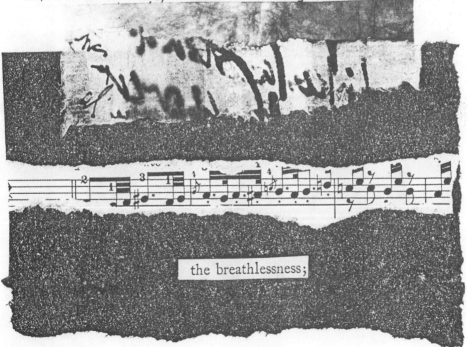

the breathlessness;

It moves around in a flowing motion.

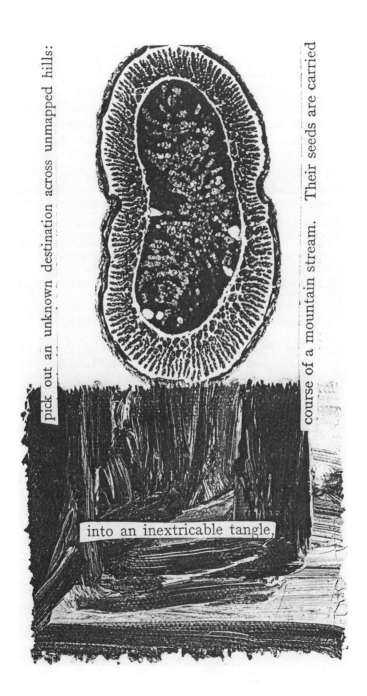

pick out an unknown destination across unmapped hills:

Their seeds are carried

course of a mountain stream.

into an inextricable tangle,

Fiona Templeton

It is hard for me to address the questions you suggest as they're rather specific to literary editing and experience of that practice. I do feel that my directorial position is more like an editor than most directors', in the Realities project, which is already a political position and one that I am sure is gender-impelled, though variations in its reception and practice do not divide at all neatly gender-wise (nor would I want them to). For me, multiplicity is not simply a quantity of the discrete, even if nominally admitted as equivalents—a very masculine notion which is feared because it undermines the security of those in power, but it does not threaten hierarchy itself. Multiplicity is relation, change and fluidity at the heart of things. Hard to assess. Assess? To sit at. One thing that has been interesting is how often the project has been reacted to as *disempowering* for me on one hand, and megalomaniac on the other (sometimes simultaneously). Personally I make no claims; I'm just *interested* in this.

Also it has been very clear that if one is to subvert one's own authority, one has to be even more lucid about expressing what, whether, and at what point one does what. About drawing boundaries, of course, which then seems authoritarian or authorial, since those inside conventions and hierarchies do not need to define positions that they only occupy by virtue of the positions that have been previously defined. The apparently strident voice of the other is only the breaking of an enforced silence; and that breaking is not the only matter.

That brings up a previous piece, "Against Agreement," a collaboration I did in 1982, where my collaborator and I discussed what we would deal with in common, though not similarly, but didn't discuss what each other were doing. "I wasn't disagreeing, I was talking about something else."

And on the subject of boundaries, another discovery of this project has been that if you simply remove a barrier (a convention) to behavior, the most common reaction is not, "Now I have a choice," but "Now there is no discrimination." This is very scary. It gives a new definition to "experimental" work, in that you have to find out, even to test, what is *tended* towards, what conventions or assumptions *remain*. So the responsibility of the collapser of genres/shifter of boundaries leaves her "sitting at" the summit table thrashing things out with what she was trying to escape from. Virilio: the idea of the tabula rasa is only a trick to deny particular absences any active value.

Fiona Templeton is writer and director of a performance project, *Realities,* consisting of interlocking playtexts, each presented by a different director; in the final *Realities* performances, the actors and designer will use the set and the stylistically different elements of the previous productions as modules in improvised order. She is also working on an editorial project, a journal of writing from mainly non-literary disciplines; each contributor, not necessarily the writer, will be interviewed by a writer from another field about the choice and its significance in terms of writing (or the significance of writing in terms of the discipline.)

Anne Waldman

Editress

Early On

I always wanted to be a writer. My mother had some anxiety about how I would live, support myself. She was divided, a frustrated writer in many ways herself, a dutiful but highly disorganized mother, an incompetent housewife & cook. The day after my first marriage she screamed at me, "So help me I'll shoot you if I find you pushing a baby carriage in 9 months!" She wanted me to "make something of my life." And it's "harder for women." At the same time she extolled the virtues of stability in marriage. "You don't want to be an 'easy' (promiscuous) woman." I founded *Angel Hair* magazine & press after a Robert Duncan poetry reading at the Berkeley Poetry Conference in 1965 with comrade New York poet Lewis Warsh I'd just met. Our mutual friend Jonathan Cott had a line, "Angel Hair sleeps with a boy in my head." I liked the gender ambiguity of "Angel Hair" and its *double entendre* as a fine pasta and the hairy white glassy Xmas tree adornment. Still in college, editor of Bennington College's literary magazine *Silo* (we were publishing Robbe-Grillet among others), active reader of contemporary poetries, ambitious with my own work, and eager to create and enter into a larger community, this venture began some lively correspondences with poets both Lewis Warsh & I admired (Levertov, Duncan, Blackburn). There were hardly any women at the Berkeley conference. Lenore Kandel stood out. I'd met Diane DiPrima when I was 17, *in situ* at the Albert Hotel in New York City with young baby, entourage, exciting books & magazines, & her own manuscripts abounding . And also in the middle of editing her own magazine (*The Floating Bear*) & producing plays. Her rooms were a kind of mystical laboratory of poetry & alchemy. I was impressed with her stamina and her seeming ability to "do it all" as a woman. Donald Allen's historic anthology of 40 poets had only 4 women in it. When I started working at The Poetry Project at its inception, as assistant to Joel Oppenheimer, one of my goals was to include more women in the program & in the publications. Carol Bergé and Diane Wakoski were actively on the premises in those days. I met Bernadette Mayer & Hannah Weiner in 1966 (my mother Frances LeFevre Waldman, then translating & pursuing her own poetry, was in a writing workshop of Bill Berkson's with them at The New School for Social Research & introduced us) and was reading their work in manuscript, also hearing them read. I'd met Joanne Kyger in San Francisco in 1967, and felt an instant bond with her writing & person. Then Alice Notley came into our lives. The sense of other women engaged in the same demanding act of writing & being a poet in what was basically, at that time, a man's world, was inspiring, encouraging. I sought them out. We were some kind of post-war fist wave. Happily this surge continues. I read more writing by women these days because there is more available.

Iovis

Editing influences my other work certainly. When time came to make a book, editing *Iovis*, an epic poem that "takes on" male energy over 300 pages long (& still continues), became a major act of arranging & rearranging, fine tuning the 23 sections. I like the flow of arrangement. I cut into my pages with scissors. I transcribe from oral presentation. The symmetries and resonances dance in my head. I can't sleep making new arrangements for the page. I see the pages—the print & spaces—fall into place. There were many other "voices" in that book, & visuals that needed attention. I dreamed the book as holy, as a simultaneity of sacred conversation and meditation, but wanted to retain also a narrative line. The prose preambles answer this need for direction for the poet to emerge as actor, protagonist—and also serve as a guide for the reader through the maze. This work was constructed as an act of argument & explanation & passion for my young son.

Kill or Cure

This recent manuscript combines credo, polemic, travel vignette, essay, with a span of poetry recent & uncollected. It went through many arrangements, non-linear. I often argue with Allen Ginsberg about his recommendation to poets to organize chronologically, systematically—the tedium of that (for me). I used to think my approach was more female.

Anthologies

Nice To See You: Homage To Ted Berrigan and *Out Of This World* were intense labors of orchestration & love. In the Poetry Project anthology I was trying to fully embrace—and in doing so became all inclusive—a scene, a history, a place, the energy of that mimeo magazine (*The World*) (started in 1966) at its most furious pace. All the writers seemed to be speaking to one another in that book, dead and alive. The book (700 pages) lived on my floor many years in an active state as I cut & pasted, discarded, organized in many versions its contents, its humors, its *rasas*. There were amazing sparks happening between the works, between the generations. There were ongoing correspondences with many of the writers inside. Ted's *Homage* also included many who were speaking to Ted Berrigan and to one another. These are important unwieldy uncompromised documents of an historic urban literary culture. I felt like a mother as I compiled them.

The Jack Kerouac School of Disembodied Poetics

We joke at the Naropa Institute about the balance of "pinks" and "blues" in our programming of the Kerouac School. But we take this need for balance seriously. So much of the what we call the "outrider" lineage involves not only the obvious male writers, but Sappho, Dickinson, H.D., Gertrude Stein. When Allen Ginsberg & I founded the school, I raised Stein as a banner (nomer) for our "academy of the future," but Kerouac had more cultural impact, and was the winner in that round. One of the "Chairs" proposed was The Emily Dickinson Chair of Silent Scribbling. We agreed on Kerouac & I slipped "disembodied" in as a tantric twist. We have as many if not more much of the time women students than men. We address women's issues regularly in our curriculum. The women students are great goads. Our gay & lesbian community is stronger at Naropa in recent years, and the Institute, as a whole, is primarily run by women. You feel it in the atmosphere the minute you enter the gate. Andrew Schelling & I have recently edited an anthology of lectures presented at the Kerouac School with close attention to this important balance. Yet *Bombay Gin*, the student-run magazine is only receiving submissions anonymously. We think this is healthy practice.

The Work

Prajna, or wisdom, in Tibetan Buddhist psychology is generally considered the feminine priciple, and *upaya*, or skillful means, the masculine principle. Both come into play in any act of life, or invention. My imaginings in words are predisposed out of a woman's body, heard in this ear, mouthed by some kind of girl-hag. But my mind frequently travels in a man's body in dreams. I'm interested in any and all magics of mind and arrangement.

Rosmarie Waldrop

One of the pleasures of having a mag or press is that it puts me in contact with what my contemporaries write. Of course this had an influence. And it can act as an antidote to isolation—and to the rampant provincialism of the U.S.

In a tangible way, it is printing, even more than editing, that has affected my own writing. Printing letterpress (especially setting poems by hand, as we did in the beginning) is so slow a process that I became extremely aware of any unnecessary "fat." It has helped make my poems leaner.

I find editing very much a *practice* which is only indirectly informed by theories. (I put it in the plural intentionally. "Theory" threatens to become a new Theology.) Of course, my reading is informed by what else I've read, by what has formed my "taste" over the years. But theoretical texts don't play a privileged part in this, for me they are less important than the context of other literary works, though probably on a par with what I read of science, history, etc. In reading mss. I try, as much as possible, to let the text come before whatever framework. I suppose here is the root of Burning Deck's eclecticism.

No, gender is not a basis for Burning Deck decisions. Some years we publish more women (1993: 4 women, 1 man), other years, more men. I must admit that I read mss. by women with extra attention, but my first commitment is to *poems.* I am sometimes bothered by the large role that happenstance plays (who sends a ms. at which moment, etc.), but prefer going with it to, say, a quota system.

Women's mags and presses have been necessary and useful, but the "ghetto"-problems are obvious. I was delighted with the first issue of *Big Allis* which, without comment, printed all women poets plus 1 male poet—a nice reversal of the usual tokenism.

I'd love to have power, but Burning Deck has such limited and uncertain means that it would be ludicrous to think in those terms. And *whose* power do you think we can subvert? *New York Times Book Review*? Adventurous writing can't, by definition, be mainstream. Can't have it both ways. I'm afraid we have to settle for long range effects and meanwhile find other ways to eat.

Obligations? Practical ones only: to do our best to read carefully, within a reasonable time, and publish the accepted work. But let's not forget this is unpaid work that we all do on top of making a living, writing our own work. So who's going to lay down obligations for me?

Rosmarie Waldrop is editor and designer for Burning Deck Books.

Julia T. Wood

I am a strong feminist and do my primary teaching and research in feminist epistemology and theory, and in gender and communication. Thus I am aware both theoretically and personally of various biases and special encumbrances faced by women in various professional roles, including editing. Even so, I have found less resistance than I would have anticipated in my editorial activities. That may be due, in part, to the fact that the role and title of editor (or associate editor reviewing a ms. for a journal) give me a certain "position power" that obligates others to respect (or at least comply with) my suggestions.

What I have found is ignorance—lots of it! By this I mean that I read so many manuscripts which are entirely innocent of feminist and/or gender research relevant to their own focus. To me this suggests that mainstream scholars continue to avoid reading articles in feminist, women's studies, and gender/sex journals. After being frustrated for some time by the absences of feminist and gender insights in manuscripts I read, I realized that these absences, coupled with my position to recommend for or against publication, provide a very important opportunity for enlarging general awareness of important scholarship in feminist and gender studies. Thus, I use my reviews to "educate" authors about gender and feminist work germane to their own foci of investigation. Often, I suggest to an author that a study would be acceptable if it were revised to acknowledge important feminist and/or gender research that strengthens the theoretical contextualization of the present study and/or suggests alternative or supplemental explanations of findings. When authors understand that their work will not be accepted if they do not include relevant work from feminist and gender scholars, they are most ready to read it and use it!

Question one: Editing books and especially a three year tenure as editor of a national journal substantially cuts into time for my own research. It is a major commitment of time and energy. I am doing it because I think all professionals owe some citizenship duty to their fields, which means taking on responsibilities that involve service to the field as a whole.

Question two: I don't think gender plays a particularly substantial role in my editorial practice. My feminist knowledge and allegiances, however, do. In the preceding paragraphs I spelled out some of the ways in which those influence how I read submissions and comment on them, as well as how I select reviewers for my journal.

Your third question is whether editing is power or subversion of power. In my judgment, it is clearly a powerful role—editors are gatekeepers, deciding what is published and, thus, what constitutes the literature of a field. A primary way editors do this is by selecting reviewers (or associate editors) for journals and edited books. The editorial board for my journal consists of an equal number of women and men, and most of both sexes have some understanding of gender issues, sexist biases, and feminist scholarship. This guarantees that those issues will affect how the reviewers read and judge manuscripts submitted to the journal. It also establishes a number of women as gatekeepers for the scholarship of a field.

Question 4: I see my primary obligation as editing a journal that includes scholarship of interest to my entire field. This means, for instance, that I cannot turn my journal into a feminist one when that is not its defined mission. I can and do make sure that feminist understandings infuse the review process, but I do not and will not publish a disproportionate number of pieces of interest to any one group, including women and/or feminist and gender scholars. That would violate my trust as editor.

Question 6: Women's writing per se has not necessarily been marginalized. However, research on women and/or research emanating from feminist modes of inquiry has been unrelentingly marginalized. This has been and continues to be a problem. As I indicated above, I try to change this by pointing authors of studies to feminist/gender research they have overlooked and must cite in order for me to recommend publication of their work. In addition, I make sure that my editorial board includes a majority of members who are open to non-traditional topics and methods of inquiry.

Question 7: I believe I have answered in the above comments. To those remarks I would add that I think (hope) I am more sensitive to the *process* of editing than some of the editors (usually, but not invariably male) with whom I have worked. I spend inordinate amounts of time composing letters to authors, especially when I must inform them that I am not accepting a paper they submitted. Unlike the letters I have frequently seen from other editors, I try to do more than simply render a decision on content; I also attempt to deal with the human being(s) who wrote papers. Thus, I endeavor to note what is strong and good about their work and to suggest ways they might develop their ideas more strongly for future submissions to my journal or other fora.

I'm sure that what I've written here opens as many questions as it answers. Perhaps that is the idea behind your innovative format of "chains." Please feel free to contact me further to continue this dialogue.

Julia T. Wood has co-edited two university press books, and is currently co-editing three other books aimed for scholars (i.e., not textbooks). In addition, she is an editorial board member and manuscript reviewer for four national journals. In November of 1993 she was selected as editor of the *Journal of Applied Communication Research*, which is one of six journals sponsored by the National Association of Communication.

Katie Yates

Dear Juliana and Jena:

You may use this statement about gender and editing though I am certain it does not honor the rules and regulations of *the* discourse which I realize in this stage of 3rd Wave Feminism is quite sophisticated, agenda-ridden . . . calls for a lexicon . . .

Since your call for submissions in early August, I have been bantering around, trying to tie into the rhetorics of Feminisms and Poetries and editing practices that may herein coincide. My search located only a series of experiences (relationships) with men, women who are poets, editors. Each one varies in circumstance, in level of maturity, is often contingent on what we have read, though the single most important discussion for me becomes what the poem is for and who the poem is to. This is my personal search.

In terms of working on *Thirteenth Moon*, I've found a certain decisiveness involved with soliciting work from women writers, that I put aside critical contingencies, am willing to accept a dialogue with a woman who writes whether she is submitting her first piece of writing ever or is well-along a continuum which identifies us as poets, people, women with a serious concern for what is said and how it is said and called a poem.

My intuition is that any of the given number of communities of writers that I am aware of whether they are affiliated with a school or are defined more by an oral tradition, performance, will benefit from the establishment of a press, a performance series which focuses on women's work. I am prepared to take such steps when I am finished with my work in graduate school.

This is about as radical as I get.

My notes on editing & (to gender, ?)

Needing to select the relationship with the writer, be thoughtful, committed to talking, listening inside and outside of the formal constraints of defining, deciding the whethers of the poetry like in each article as it speaks. How do we want to be spoken to, how to consummate a relationship in words: sequin by sequin each night.

Poems as women who are not separate from building; dense; attracted to and in the arboretum.

"handle nouns with me," she asks, for example I want to review Elizabeth's book.

 I do, I begin: i e m a n j e = bareheaded
  : there is no "to be"
  : firm tryst skilsaw
  : how(e)
  : subtle be estranged and at what cost kindness
 palms: to hand over
 poetry could become feminine

Transcript of "Ethics of Small Press Publishing"

On March 31–April 3, 1993, Writing from the New Coast: First Festival of Poetry was held at the State University of New York at Buffalo. The event was curated by Peter Gizzi and Juliana Spahr. We have reproduced here selections from the "Ethics of Small Press Publishing" panel. The panel was moderated by Jefferson Hansen, editor of *Poetic Briefs*, and featured Lee Ann Brown, editor of Tender Buttons Press, Cydney Chadwick, editor of *Avec*, Connell McGrath, editor of *o-blek*, Gale Nelson, editor of Paradigm Press, and Rod Smith, editor of *Aerial*. Most of the audience members also had significant experience as editors and/or curators. The panelists each read a brief statement about editing (most of these are reproduced in *Writing from the New Coast: Technique*, volume two of *o-blek*/12). We have reproduced the conversation surrounding this panel because it was very influential to our thinking about how to create a journal that might be in some way opposed to conventional editorial decision making.

Brown, at the end of her presentation, did an unannounced performance with various audience members of Robert Duncan's "A Fairie Play: A Play." This transcript starts immediately after this performance.

Q: Tell us what it [the performance of "A Fairie Play: A Play"] has to do with publishing?

Brown: It has to do with presenting the work, that's the main reason I do this is to get the work out. When I realized I could make a book happen, when Bernadette Mayer had her sonnets sitting in a drawer for a long time and she tried to get them published in a few places, I was like I could do this you know, I could just make it happen and make it be a real book. I could just send it to the printer and it would come back and it would be a real thing. Then I could give it to people or sell it. It would just make the work be realized in the world. I would love to do Tender Albums, Tender Broadsides, Tender Everything, you know what I mean.

Hansen: And now Connell McGrath of *o-blek* . . .

McGrath: I'm going to speak for myself and use "I" although

I'm sure Peter [Gizzi, co-editor of *o-blek* with McGrath] agrees with what I have to say I'll let him speak for himself. The principles behind *o-blek* are that we try to present work as faithfully as possible according to typescript. The second principle is that we try to exclusively accept work only on the basis of our own taste. I find I've seen in the past a lot of publications that operate in terms of trying to represent something or do something specific and I think that that's fine but I think that the most powerful things I've seen are things that admit personal taste as the only basis to make that decision on. Those are the two principles, the only things that I can really see that we do. We wanted to make something beautiful and to honor the poets that appear in our pages and that's really what the title pages[1] are about. We are trying to find some kind of a gender balance and I bring this up because it's true and because I want to reintroduce the question that we didn't get to yesterday at the end of our panel, of the last panel yesterday.[2] We've been concerned with gender balance. Most issues of *o-blek* tend to have more men than women and I don't have any excuse for that really. I'm interested in seeing magazines that are devoted exclusively to women's work and I understand the need for that. Certainly there have been enough magazines devoted to men's work in the past whether intentional or not and some kind of an action is being taken to correct the balance and I want to open up that to discussion and try to pick up as I said where we left off yesterday in the discussion of gender and representation in publications and in forums. The other difficulty we have is sales . . .

Jonathan Fernandez: You said that you publish on the basis of taste and then you went on to say something about the balance of men versus women, or say blacks vs. whites, or whatever, in the magazine. Would you agree that your taste runs mainly to men's writings and that you have some perception in yourself that you know something about men's writing for some reason or do you mean that it is a matter of submissions? You get so many submissions from men and so few from women and it just ends up that way?

McGrath: I think the balance of submissions is a factor. I haven't

---

[1] The format of *o-blek* is to present each author's name and poem title on an independent page preceding the work.

[2] A discussion of gender politics at the end of the previous day's "Reading and Refiguring" panel was cut short due to time limitations.

really looked at the numbers but certainly in putting this last issue together I've been a little more aware of it than usual and it does seem that we get more submissions from men and I don't really understand that because I believe that there are an equal number of women writing as men. As for our taste, perhaps, certainly the evidence would suggest, seeing as we publish more men than women, that somehow we're connecting more with that and I can't make a value judgment on that.

Chadwick: I've been doing *Avec* for 5 years now and I get more submissions from men. Women have to be asked for it, they just don't send it out the way men do. And with *Avec* I don't try to do 50/50. I just take whatever work I want to publish but there's always more men because they're the ones who send the work. And then the pages fill, I look at the roster and usually count because I'm curious and there are always more men.

Jessica Grim:[3] *Big Allis* gets more submissions from men.

Mark Wallace:[4] From women?

Grim: I said from men, and that's not quite true but we get equal numbers even though we predominantly publish women.

Thad Ziolkowski: I just want to commend Connell for confessing to the taste factor and I'd like other people to address it because it's an interesting problem. I guess I just want to pose that problem to the whole panel to see if that could be investigated a little more. It [taste] seems to be the vanishing point of ethics questions and it is the place where a lot of the ethics questions can disappear or can be brought into focus against that background.

Hansen: Yeah, why do we like what we like?

Ziolkowski: But I'd like to keep it from devolving around the niceties around the problem of taste itself, which is so mysterious, but instead see it as an operative principle within publishing. I don't know, there's a kind of epistemology of taste but then there's publishing around taste you know.

---

[3] Jessica Grim edits *Big Allis* with Melanie Neilson.
[4] Mark Wallace is editor of *Situation* and co-editor of Leave Books.

Hansen: Yeah, I see what you mean.

McGrath: I would like to actually clarify a little bit my position on taste. What I see happening for us is that we can get side-tracked, I can get sidetracked by questions of fame, for instance, if so and so is a good poet—you [to Hansen] did a little thing in the story that Mr. Schmo sent in about a famous poet sending in a bad poem and publishing it anyway and there's enormous temptation in that and we try not to do it. Sometimes we do do it anyway. And then there are also other considerations, considerations of friendship, anyone who's been an editor for any amount of time knows it's easy to hurt people's feelings and make enemies and I don't like to do that myself but it happens anyway. So there are other considerations that seem to sidetrack me from this principle.

Randall Potts: Do you ever fantasize about anonymity, as if it would be ideal if your name weren't attached to it and you could produce this thing without having a location and no one would know who was doing it and you wouldn't have that sense of the network of friends—

Rod Smith: —the Satanic Verses paperback was done in that manner. The address for the publisher was an empty office in Vermont. *(laughter)*

Potts: That's the only thing I think about where the publisher doesn't acknowledge . . .

Miekal And:[5] There are underground things . . . a group of people publish under the name of Karen Eliot and they all publish magazines called *Smile*. There's a collection of fifty up to one hundred magazines called *Smile* and they're published all over the world.

Smith: Actually I've gotten that in the mail.

McGrath: I haven't considered that but I've considered something else which is having all contributors be anonymous. *(laughter)* I don't think that most poets would go for that though. *(more laughter)*

---

[5] Miekal And is the editor, with Liz Was, of Xexoxial Editions.

Q: Too bad though, to give up our rights to have individual taste I think that adds a vibrancy and a personality. As if there could be some objective fairness that a poet or a poem meets.

Juliana Spahr: I think that we need to be talking to Lee Ann and Cydney about these issues. I also find it upsetting that when we talk about these things—like famous poets and bad poems—it always seems that these exceptions aren't made for women. I think this is happening because there aren't enough women editing. So maybe you guys [to Brown and Chadwick] would be willing to talk about that.

Brown: I have a problem with the word "taste" anyway because "good taste" is very high class sounding. The way I approach it is first of all to publish the people who were inspiring to me as a poet and they happen to be women. I didn't really interrogate that thoroughly at first. But as I have begun to perceive it and question whether I should only publish women or not, I feel comfortable with staying with that decision even though I made some exceptions with the broadsides just now.·[6] There are so many great women writing that I'm never going to run out even if I get a million dollars. This new generation right now is really amazing. I always make these lists of if I could have my fantasy who I would publish and I just made another list today: Kim Lyons, Wanda Phipps, Andrea Hollowell, Melanie Neilson, Wang Ping, Helena Bennett, Katie Yates, Euphrosyne Bloom, India Hixon, those people published in the broadsides, Stacy Doris, there's such a rich area and it's so powerful right now.

Liz Was:[7] One of the ways we dealt with this at Xexoxial Editions over the last twelve years is that we always have mail art/participation projects and invite anybody to submit and they're guaranteed that if they submit their piece will go in. Not all of our projects have an open invitation like that but we always make sure that at least one thing like that is going on. Like *The Acts The Shelf Life,* an "assembling project," and various magazines—*Anti-Isolation* and *Spek.*

---

[6] At the conference Brown had distributed a series of broadsides—one was a collaboration between Brown, Liz Fodaski, and Ted Pearson, the others featured the work of Laynie Browne, Judith Goldman, Lisa Jarnot, Jennifer Moxley, Sianne Ngai, Danine Ricerito, and James Thomas Stevens.
[7] Liz Was is the editor of Xexoxial Editions with Miekal And.

And: Like the novel . . .

Was: Right, the novel approach was a collective novel where we told people to send in parts of a novel without telling them the theme or anything and we put them all together in the order we received them and people are credited by their name at the top so that's one way of dealing with it. Is it a good novel? That begs the question. You want to talk about taste—is it good? We all admit it's a subjective thing and we all admit we have our own tastes. I'm just saying that one way practically to get around that as a publisher is to have some things that are completely open and also having your say in more selective things.

Susan Gevirtz:[8] I wanted to address this issue of taste which I feel is not arbitrary or neutral in any kind of way. I think taste always has some relationship to the canon and that's a very gendered relationship. I wonder what happens if as editor one interrogates one's own taste and considers publishing work that is interesting but not necessarily work that you like and that might be a way of investigating the authority of gender positions in doing something like that?

Smith: I would say that *Aerial* comes out of a certain tradition, a recent tradition; however you want to look at it, it has a certain direction it's pointed in but I don't consider that exclusive. I like to put in things that play off each other. You could think of it as a kind of soup or something—you have a lot of a certain recipe and you want to get something else or you don't need quite as much of it, but it plays off and it makes something. Picasso said a bad painting hanging among good paintings will look good and a good painting hanging among bad paintings will look bad. I think that's a way of thinking about the process of editing.

Gevirtz: But when you say the word "direction" it makes me think of diagnosis.

Smith: Diagnosis?

Gevirtz: Yeah, the way that the position of editor is deciding a direction is also a position of decision about—

---

8 Susan Gevirtz was the editor of *HOW(ever)*.

Smith: Well, yeah . . . that's another way to talk about the economics. For example, my wife [Gretchen Johnson] is carrying over fifty thousand dollars worth of credit card debt for a magazine she did called *Gargoyle* and that stopped in 1987. So to criticize her and what she chose to put in that magazine seems ridiculous. This is something you choose to do yourself and you choose to take the consequences of it and you choose to spend your own money on it. You have to remember that.

McGrath: And some of the consequence is criticism.

Smith: Yeah, well that's more interesting than carrying debt. *(laughter)*

Wallace: I wanted to return briefly to the two things that are moving in and out of each other—one is the issue of taste and the other is of gender. I think there's a complicated interrelation here. I'm not objecting to the idea of taste in the sense you were saying. I prefer to drink a wine that tastes better than one that doesn't. But when you talk about taste you already have to recognize it in the first place, so you're dealing with social constructions of identity and situations in the first place. So it seems to be pretty clear that taste is influenced by those sorts of attitudes. I've got a little display over here I'm doing of Leave Books, Jeff's magazine *Poetic Briefs* and the thing I do, *Situation*, and in one issue of *Poetic Briefs* we published a letter that was sent to us by Clayton Eshleman about the Leave Books project in which he called them "ephemeral slim little darlings."[9] Now on the one hand you could say well hey that's just his taste right, you know, on the other hand, and it is [his taste], no one suspects him of dishonesty in being inclined toward big bushy magazines with lots of staples. But at the same time it's clear that his taste has been structured by highly questionable and problematic social dynamics. That I think is where the interrelation lies and that's why along with one's right to assert one's taste also comes the necessity to challenge the sense of one's own taste. I mean, where do you get it from, you know?

Smith: (holding up issue of *Aerial/5*) I was aware in putting this issue together in particular, but I'm not sure, that it's because I liked the writing, I mean there's 40 pages of Carla Harryman's and Lyn Hejinian's "A Wide Road" in here, there's a long

---

[9] See *Poetic Briefs* 1:6, 1992.

interview with Tina Darragh by Joan Retallack, there's a long essay on Cage by Joan Retallack in here, also Gretchen Johnson, Elaine Equi, Susan Smith Nash. It's just that I liked the writing, that's why I published it. I don't know, I believe I have counted *Aerial 6/7* and I think there are more men in it and the next two issues are going to be more heavily male centered because they're special issues on male figures—issue 8 on Barrett Watten and 9 on Bruce Andrews—and that's the way it happened, but they're not exclusively male by any means.

Melanie Neilson:[10] You can correct me if I'm wrong, but as I understand it you made an attempt to solicit essays from many women but more men responded, is that right? And I just want to mention that because I think it's really important. Women should be more active.

Daniel Davidson: I've done a lot of curating in San Francisco and my gut feeling is that when you enter the public sphere, producing work that is consumed by a large population or small population, the responsibility sloughs off from one's own specific necessities and there must be a social concern larger than one's own private interests. That wasn't a perspective I thought out but it seems to me on the surface an obvious fact, to conduct yourself in a public arena and to ask for public inclusion and to say that you have some hegemonic control dictated by your own spurious needs however they may be acquired is ridiculous. My view is that, I have never done otherwise. Every reading I've ever done has always been fifty percent women. I don't think any other course of behavior where a reading series is concerned is considered viable. What I would like to ask in terms of publishing is the difference between say Peter Ganick's most current project,[11] which is twenty-three women and twenty-two men, if there's any problem with that. Does anyone have a problem with actually slotting a fifty-fifty split with one more proviso? Personally, I think the most interesting writing as, a gross generality in contemporary poetics, is by women. I don't see why magazines are not at least fifty percent women, I just don't understand it.

Smith: I don't have a problem with that but I prefer to think of

[10] Melanie Neilson edits *Big Allis* with Jessica Grim.

[11] Davidson is referring here to *The Art of Practice: 45 Contemporary Poets*, ed. Dennis Barone and Peter Ganick, Elmwood: Potes & Poets, 1994.

editing as a process like I said, like a soup, so I don't like to count.

McGrath: Also, there is a significant difference between doing a reading series and a magazine. There's something, for me, something much more organic about editing a magazine than a reading series

Smith: Have you ever done a reading series?

McGrath: Um, Yes. In a reading series, as I experience it, one decides who one wants to read and then asks.

Davidson: It's a question of taste, the same as you evidenced for publishing decisions. I like certain writers more than others but I don't . . .

Nelson: Small presses are small and we make the community and in Rhode Island there are a number of small presses: Lost Roads, Tender Buttons, one of the grandparents of small presses, Burning Deck, Paradigm Press, Copper Beech, a number of magazines, *The Impercipient*, *Black Bread*, it's a community and we are all doing something and we do what we can, we make books. I love the stacks of papers and putting them into books and different people have different takes and we all are doing something as one can see in the amount of people here working on magazines or doing something in a poetic context. To me Paradigm is this tiny little thing, I mean I care about it, I put my money, my life into it, but most of you don't care about paradigm press, you'll leave here today and say, oh, that was nice, but you, quite honestly, don't care about it in that sense. At least that's my perception of it, I mean I like to see books from other places and I like some presses more than others and I'm always delighted to be surprised and excited but I don't really care. This may sound really stupid and close-minded, but I don't really care what got the press or the magazine to do what, but if the work is interesting and beautiful, I'm going to read it. Maybe I'm just out somewhere, confused by this conversation, but it doesn't occur to me. I bring out books.

Grim: I just wanted to say what if the situation were reversed? This issue of social responsibility and tokenism and half and half—these things are really problematic issues that are important. I don't think that there is an easy solution. One thing I was thinking of was, reverse that situation—if we were living in a matriarchal society, would the women turn around and say oh the men are under–represented in the magazines, we better make sure they get in there? I don't know. And what would that be like? How would men feel if their representation was based on that fact that they were downtrodden, that they needed some help.

Smith: The thing Dan said the other day about how power is taken. I mean, take the power.

Grim: Yes, exactly.

C.S. Giscombe:[12] I wanted to comment also on the idea of the invisible center of taste, which has been brought up here rather often. What I would think is that a press, or perhaps a literary journal, is less a cornerstone perhaps, less a monolith. There's a dialogue in a very public place of engagement in which the issues of the literary world, things like taste, gender, race, are necessarily engaged by the public and by the writers and the readers because all those things, very much like the public journal, exist for themselves in the world. This is not a place that we as editors can hide from. We can't hide behind the magazine; there's not an easy answer, but there are a series of hard questions, real hard back and forths that I think are part of what the process of publishing is about.

---

[12] C.S. Giscombe is a former editor of *Epoch*.

Editors' Notes: Frameworks

Relation: Perhaps a good starting point would be to discuss my apprehension about editing. I am uncomfortable with the idea of the editor as arbiter of good taste, or as the (in)visible navigator/sculptor of a final packaged product. Journals rarely seem to openly admit the presence of personal ideology behind their pages. And when they do, the "personalized" frame seems to stifle and alter the work by mashing it into an overly-prescribed space. We all change what we read in the very act of reading; however, editing forces an external median strip between the substance of the original and what it will become. Such mediation can create a powerfully dialogic space; it can also create a "culinary" space that limits the possibilities in the act of reading. The *Chain* project is an attempt to investigate the (im)possibility of an unmediated reception, the (im)possibility of detaching a writing from its presentational/ideological form.

Relation: I edited an anthology earlier in the year and at the end of that, despite the fact that I spent a year reading for it and thinking about the politics of representation in its construction, the final product left me alienated and confused. This confusion was not predicated on a lack of faith in the authors represented in the collection, but on the ability of any collection to make claims of authority or finality or even of representation (which anthologies claim by their very definition). While I still don't feel we've escaped authority's claims in this format, I feel farther away from the product, detached as it were, from my claims.

Part One: Editorial Forum

Production: It is impossible to make a frameless frame (although that is the vision from which this project derived). We have instead begun the journal with a forum that takes a look at how and why journals are created and in what ways questions of gender have informed those decisions. It sounds absurd to edit a journal that's about the editing of journals—a nightmare of self-reflexivity—and yet it is a way of creating a body that shows its own skeleton. Instead of putting together a collection that claims over and over the ability of the editor to know and define ("hey! great outfit!"), we wanted to be able to say "this made itself and here is what it's made of; it is just a part of what continues." This is not to say that there aren't editors out there rejecting the role of objective talent scout—in fact there are many editors who will quickly admit that their personal taste is responsible for what they publish—but does that release the work from questioning the taste that lead to its appearance? What are the implications behind making a personal taste public? Why not simply enjoy that taste (or idea) in a more private way? The manner in which taste presents itself in the public sphere is something always worth examining.

Susan Smith Nash: Feminist theory has helped me a great deal by giving me a vocabulary of "influence-rearrangement" (I prefer this catch-phrase to ones that rely on the word "power"; that word is too reductive)

[Brecht used a half-curtain in his performances so that you knew the scene was over, but you could see the scene being changed. No magic, no Hollywood, no illusions that there is such a thing as seamlessness, that there's an appropriate time to suspend your disbelief. In creating the structure that we have for *Chain*, we're attempting an editorial equivalent of the half-curtain.]

Chain does not escape the problem of private concerns displaying themselves publicly (not that any presentation could escape this problem), as is evident from the journal's structure, as well as our decision to include only women writers in the journal. This was not an easy decision; we are both aware of the difficulties of talking about gender as in any way other than constructed. To start a gender-centered forum is in some ways reinstating problematic narratives of gender. The spectre of separatism looms large. Our frame has separated out (in the manner that elements are distilled out from a liquid concentrate) an issue (gender and editing) that is discursive. The interconnection between creative word and issue orientation leads to uneasy relations. It necessitates statements which seem like they are meant to stand eternal—a permanent lens.

Maxine Chernoff: But the mind is everyone's home, male and female alike. The writers of our time who will be important in retrospect give full reign to the most lively of dwelling places.

Women who edit hold a particular place in an established discourse of authority Whether they think about it or not, they must evaluate their stance in relation to that realm. Perhaps to ignore that factor is in itself a form of subversion—it's a way of maintaining a frame that refuses to participate in unpleasant histories.

It is ironic that in order for dialogue to take place, conversational limits must be set. We chose the limit of gender. A conversation that takes place in print, as opposed to verbally, insists on an even further set of boundaries. Many of the elements that feed verbal scenes (body language, voice tone, immediacy, constant revision) are completely absent. However, any printed text is a gesture toward conversation; it's a presentation that invites response. We're trying to create a forum that takes that invitation seriously, that is not just going through the motions of what it means to instigate response; it *requires* continuation.

Susan Gevirtz: It would be an error to think that the woman question debates have ended. It would be an error to think we are not all inheritors . . . It would be an error to think you have finished imagining your own history.

There is a journal called *Art/Life: Communication for the Creative Mind*. Its deadline is the 15th of every month. In order to be in it, all you have to do is create a page of art and reproduce it 100 times. All the various pieces are then collated into 100 editions of the magazine. It is ironic that the "communicative" aspect of this journal is countered by the fact that it is an extremely limited edition. And for some reason the editors charge $50 for each issue. Is that communication?

We did not succeed in creating a form by which the journal could spontaneously combust. Our initial solicitation of both editors and poets overly-determined the membership of these pages' community, another example of how conversation is contingent on a restrictive foundation. Conversations must take place in a locale, and not everyone can exist at one single moment in one locale—although ideally, all voices would have an opportunity to enter the room and make the changes they deemed necessary to their concerns. Our concerns included the desire for more communication with women writers than our current locale allows for.

Production: While *Chain* is an attempt at a conversational journal, any editor must make choices. Our choices were of format. We wanted somehow to create a journal free of the constrictions and assumptions of "taste." But at the same time we wanted the journal to have a center. Our particular compromise is the mix of the chain letter format where we chose, more on the basis of geographical location than anything else, a number of poets to start chains; those poets in turn decided who to send their poem to for response, who then sent their poem on, etc. The intent of our format was to open up the journal to other writers whose work we might not know. It has been successful at this. It is not a completely open-ended rejection of editorial prerogative such as the "assembling projects" that Liz Was mentions in the "Small Press Forum" [see *Transcript of Small Press Panel* above], but rather someplace in between.

Interjection: I disagree with the idea that we've been "successful" at opening up the journal to unfamiliar voices. Or at least it hasn't happened to the degree that we had hoped for when we came up with the concept. Writers we

Relation: When I was at Brown, a group of women visual artists did a collaborative project. They had a studio in the art building and each of the five had the room alone in five hour shifts. There was someone there 24 hours a day. You could bring whatever you wanted in and take whatever you wanted out. Anything that someone else made could be added onto or taken apart (a model for how this particular essay was put together). There were cameras in each corner of the room, as well as a free-floating camera to chart all the changes. You couldn't get too attached to what you produced because there was a good chance it would disappear/transform beyond recognition in a very short time. There was a typewriter on a table where the artists kept a sort of written record of what was happening. One day the typewriter was suspended from the ceiling. The focus of that instrument switched its function in mid-air. I like this project as a trope for public presentation of language. Anti-static, conversational, argumentative. Shifting beyond intention, forced to respond to the voices surrounding.

were less familiar with were more hesitant to respond. Or writers whom we were depending on to introduce us to new poets ignored our request for work in the way that many of us ignore the requests made by actual chain letters. Any suggestions on how to get beyond this stumbling block would be much appreciated . . .

WITH LOVE ALL THINGS ARE POSSIBLE. THIS PAPER HAS BEEN SENT TO YOU FOR GOOD LUCK. THE ORIGINAL IS IN NEW ENGLAND. IT HAS BEEN AROUND THE WORLD NINE TIMES. THE LUCK HAS BEEN SENT TO YOU. YOU WILL RECEIVE GOOD LUCK WITHIN FOUR DAYS OF RECEIVING THIS LETTER, PROVIDED IN TURN YOU SENT IT ON. THIS IS NO JOKE.

. . . How can the poems inside a structure activate their own juxtapositions, their own presentational form? How can they lose the slick editorial veneer of self-containment and become interactive? In *Chain* we conceived of an arbitrary spiral that spins loosely out from the work to include another—arbitrary in that a spiral's geometry is a fixed set of coordinates moving in a direction, but the nature of those coordinates is unknown. There is certainly a framework to create the substance's posture/being, but a framework of inclusion. The spiral is a curling around, the motion of the arm winding in, as opposed to fingers plucking and sorting . . . what geometric form would that be? Points on a line? The spiral is a figure without telos really, for its expansion outward is continuous, only momentarily frozen by the fact of its publication.

Relation: A chain rhyme is a poetic form where the last syllable of a line is repeated in the first syllable of the next line. The repeated syllable must carry a different meaning. This is how our chains work.

Linked forms are places for conversation, for a (to some extent) non-hierarchical development to occur. Such development is almost always missing from editorial considerations.

Interjection: Or are they simply moments of perplexity? lacking finality and/or charm?

Chain letters are acts of will; they are propelled by desire for luck, desire for money, fear. We might not know where they originate. We might not know where they end up. They are disposable—but with an edge.

They dredge up a side of you, the side that thinks "but what if I don't. . . . " and you can't place your resentment of having to make a decision on any one particular subject: a con-

Relation: I always throw these letters away. But before I do, I let them sit for a long time, well beyond their expiration date.

sequence of relation. This is a chain after all, a unit consisting of many, each part of equal importance, each part leading to this moment where all is contingent on your response. *Chain* attempts to take this device in a further direction. The receiver alters the nature of the chain as it is propelled forward (by desire for luck? by desire for money? by fear?). And the chain's course is tracked, the map of its passage marked in book format.

YOU WILL RECEIVE GOOD LUCK IN THE MAIL. SEND NO MONEY, AS FAITH HAS NO PRICE. DO NOT KEEP THIS LETTER. IT MUST LEAVE YOUR HANDS WITHIN 96 HOURS. AN R.A.F. OFFICER RECEIVED $170,000. JOE ELLIOT RECEIVED $40,000 AND LOST IT BECAUSE HE BROKE THE CHAIN. WHILE IN THE PHILLIPINES, GEORGE WELCH LOST HIS WIFE 51 DAYS AFTER RECEIVING THE LETTER. HE FAILED TO CIRCULATE THE LETTER.

The chain letter is a skewed form of communication. But once it is out there, it is up to each receiver to determine its fate.

Is this like reading?

DYLAN FAIRCHILD RECEIVED THE LETTER, AND NOT BELIEVING, HE THREW THE LETTER AWAY. NINE DAYS LATER HE DIED.

Chains

Dear Poet,

We are currently requesting work for a new journal called *Chain*, devoted to the work of women poets, editors and critics. The journal will consist of two parts: a critical forum on editorial practices and a series of "chains"/poems and other responses that enact an alternative editorial practice.

Chain letters are a form of twisted communication that we hope to appropriate in order to structure an active forum for women's writing. We're asking for work from people in different parts of the U.S. and Canada. We hope to use this forum to investigate an alternative editing practice while simultaneously questioning those aspects of editing that are usually taken for granted (i.e. editor as invisible mover and shaker, editor as definer of aesthetic—"I only print the work I like," editor as autocrat). Thus, we ask you to follow the following guidelines for submission:

The journal will consist of a number of series. A series may be as short as two poems in response to each other, or as large as five poems also in response. We have randomly selected poets to begin each series; we don't view this as a solicitation, but as a request that will ultimately bring together a broad range of work in the final product. We are asking you to write a poem that will begin a series, or, if you are not able, to forward this letter to someone who will. After your poem is written, please send it on, along with this letter, to a woman poet whose work you're interested in. That second writer will write a poem in "response" to yours. The second writer will send the two poems on to a third writer, etc., until the chain is completed (see below for length of chain). Please be aware that each author will probably be limited to five pages of printed matter. If your poem exceeds this limit, you should suggest which sections you would like to see in print.

As we know, chain letters are often broken. In order not to lose remarkable "links," we would appreciate that each writer send a copy of her particular poem to us. Include the name of the person from whom you received the "solicitation," and the name of the person you sent the series on to. Of course, if your poem is the last link on the chain, send all of the poems in the series back to us. If you receive this letter and are not able to respond, please send the letter on to another poet so that the chain will not be broken. You should not hold on to this letter for more than three weeks.

This letter will bring you good luck.

Sincerely,

Juliana Spahr   Jena Osman

Sherry Brennan

Julia Blumenreich

H.T.

Susan Smith Nash

Lisa Houston

Domestic Bliss/Dominus Patrus

i

Days go by
home seems further

> We buttress it anew with every generation; we love its very
> cracks and crumbling corners; we hang and drape it with
> endless decorations. (Gilman 205)

'pared out of papure'
say so

we crawled along
a dark bridge

'abide in my love'
too close to home today

myself, the home

ii

The daily means no danger to me.

Towards me. The danger comes towards.
And it comes unexpectedly. Or it will come.

From without. without the limits.
of the daily. either in the night.

Sherry Brennan to Julia Blumenreich

or irregularly. or seldom.
or as the unique line, which cuts

across the refraining boundary
without repetition and without a sign

and without warning
or just from without

I repeat myself to refrain from danger
I stammer to keep it from you

to keep my danger from you
thus I manage to refrain myself from you

and you can keep yourself
without the danger which I

pose so repetitively that you
will only recognize daily

doings, like mending socks or washing
or baking a breakfast roll.

You will not hear the danger.
It has been daily. Without me.

iii

He cleaned his father's house
shooing the animals out with a whip

out of my father's house
took that whip

zeal of the Lord of Hosts has eaten
me up

[1]do.mes.tic \de-mes-tik\ adj[MF domestique, fr. L domesticus, fr. domus] 1 : of or relating to the household or the family 2 : of, relating to, or carried on within one and esp. one's own country <~ politics> <~ wines> 3: INDIGENOUS 4 a : living near or about the habitations of man b : TAME, DOMESTICATED 5 : devoted to home duties and pleasures. (Webster's)

domain (de´main, deu-) sb. . . . . for earlier F. demaine, OF. demeine:—L. dominicum. in med. L. ='proprietas, quod ad dominum spectat', subst. use of dominicus of or belonging to a lord, of the nature of private property, proper, own. (OED)

'Dominium eminens, quod civitas habet in cives et res civium, ad usum publicum.'

'He was lord of his library and seldom cared for looking out beyond his domains.'

domestic (de´mestik, deu-), a. and sb. . . . [ad. L. domestic-us, f. domus house: see DOME. (OED)

'All domesticable animals of any note have long fallen under the yoke of man.'

domesticate (de´mestikeit, due-), v. [f. ppl. stem of med.L. domesticare to dwell in a house, to accustom (Du Cange), f. domestic-us DOMESTIC. (OED)

'Ireland, where the wisedome and valour of the Duke of Yorke had domesticated a savage people.'

'Childbed *matronizes* the giddiest Spirits . . . it *domesticates* her, as I may say.'

doubtless a romantic piquancy in the discovery that a young woman was engaged in such adventures of scholarship, and it might certainly have been enhanced by a glance at the strange domestic interior in which they were conducted. (English Scholars 72-3)

'who so proper to
play the Criticks

in this as the Females'
'surrounded by books

and dirtiness'
'a revealing privacy'

'too much the drug called learning'
'neglect their household Affairs'

'strange career'
'as his 'Saxon Mistress"

'without ever herself attaining
to the front rank in scholarship'

'no need to overrate'
'the Saxon nymph'

'governess' 'I wear no
other stockings

but what I knit myself'

vi

The total work carried out by women who make clothes at home is considered to be more (two *jornales*) than that of women who labor only in workshops ("you have only one thing to do"). The amount of work done by women making clothes at home is thought to be exceeded only by women who labor in workshops and also take care of domestic chores at home afterward. (There was no such case in the village studied.) (Narotzky 82)

'Ah, the women' 'For God and HOME
and NATIVE LAND' 'domestic joy'

'Cooking and laundry, and hygiene—
domestic science it's called' 'to feel

"at home"; to familiarize'
'afterwards we make tortillas by hand'

'When one finishes with the kitchen chores'
'I don't get distracted because if I do,

it's to do other chores' 'devotion to home'
'When I'm sewing, I remember that upstairs

the beds are still unmade. And, alas,
there's this huge amount of clothing that must be mended.

That is to say, I accumulate this huge amount of things
in my head.' 'my body never rests'

'It's that it is an additional burden, that is,'
Or ... 'by taking care of my husband and my children,

I have already earned a day's wages.' 'And to this one adds
another job.' 'it's not possible to do two day's work—

but a woman does.' 'double day'
'If we had land we would stop weaving'

vii
     A three course meal has more 'value' in domestic terms
     than a quick snack, a carefully ironed shirt more than one
     pulled directly from the tumble drier. (cited in Collins
     21)

It's a question of value. In Cynthia Woodsong and Randall H.
McGuire's study of Binghampton, New York between 1930
and 1980, "Making Ends Meet," the discrepancy in the ways

waged and unwaged work are assigned dollar values creates a difficulty for the comparison of men's and women's work. Their solution is to count and compare equally any hour of labor rather than the market value ascribed to that hour. So that "income" is defined in the essay as the hours of labor contributed (rather than dollars earned) to the family. According to this definition, by the 1970's, in the average family of four, women were contributing 20% more "income" than men, most of it un- or underpaid. Woodsong and McGuire do not go on to quantify the comparative dollar values of men's and women's labor, but if they did, one could determine the extent to which women's work has been undervalued in the labor market.

> she had thought there was a poetry in such passion beyond any to be found in everyday domesticity. (Eliot Chap 42)

In coming to terms with her life of everyday domesticity, George Eliot's character questions the way she had valued a rhetoric or poetics of passion in her youth. This poem presents a similar linguistic dilemma of evaluation for me. I have accumulated a mass of language on the issue of domesticity—marxist and feminist analyses, statistics, quotations of working women discussing their own domestication, roots, derivations, usage—but this mass does not constitute a poetry. And I ask myself whether my role as the poet is to give this material value—to domesticate it, dominate it, take it as my proper domain—and render it poetic?

viii

> We don't figure our accounts with a pencil and paper, but we do make an accounting in our heads of the cloth and the thread. It figures out to be a gift. There are no earnings. Our work is given as a gift. (Cook 111)

> Our Poet's gift in raising it into the domain of Art. (Carlyle, cited in OED)

> And your words (Domestickes to you) serve your will. (Shakespeare, cited in OED)

'on both a daily and a generational basis'
'reproduction' 'making' in Chaucer's terms

another man's garden of metaphors
becomes my poem

'a home which is no home'

Resources
Jane L. Collins, and Martha Gimenez, eds., *Work Without Wages: Domestic Labor and Self-Employment within Capitalism*. Scott Cook, "Female Labor, Commodity Production, and Ideology in Mexican Peasant-Artisan Households," in Collins and Gimenez. *Dictionary of National Biography*, "Elizabeth Elstob." George Eliot, *Felix Holt. Gawain and the Green Knight.* Charlotte Perkins Gilman, *Women and Economics*. David C. Douglas, *English Scholars. John*, King James Version. Susana Narotzky, "'Not to be a Burden': Ideologies of the Domestic Group and Women's Work in Rural Catalonia," in Collins and Gimenez. Cynthia Woodsong and Randall H. McGuire, "Making Ends Meet: Unwaged Work and Domestic Inequality in Broome County, New York, 1930-1980," in Collins and Gimenez. All quotations in section iv from the *Oxford English Dictionary (OED)*.

When He Died

is very wrong with this animal
too sick to get up yet she
rolled over and wanted her belly rubbed.
The deed is done
old black lab chose to
can you imagine choosing to curl up, too sick to move
right in the middle of the morning schoolyard
the blacktop teeming with 800 children ages K - 8 ?

the worst is where the toes attach to the swollen feet,
the sensation is only
deserted if it's shared somehow
like the illnesses that are terminal
making us lie and offer to do something—

"call if you need me".

Told the rest of the family the house wasn't
fit for any thing other than monsters
sunny bedroom of her granddaughter
parquet-floored livingspaces,
logs in place
company's feet soothed by the fire
"a mole wouldn't even live in the basement . . ."
that hairy little animal with the penial snout passing
up the house's foundation

Julia Blumenreich to H.T.

she slept in our bed
"a good night's sleep".

I've given up no don't say that meaning could be the sound of
words like hard "c" in coughing, the mush of my tongue before
"lullaby" the "d" of the young's this and that and finger
pointing—U and u and you and ewe and yoU and yOU and
YOU.

At 35 the mother said her fourth took the last bit of her
youthful spirit outta her evenso the wash in dark wash out gray
has stayed for many months in the sock drawer
when company came and left "I had changed:
a hard year, but now he's all better, all cured?"

gesture the scramble is the same as the naked
mole rats in the reptile house in their underground "city"
never seemed to stop moving their tunnels as a birth canal
is felt then freed my daughter's arms flailed her eyes closed
then unfocused for quite some time.

humor me when I speak of chameleon language we command
after all "I am haunted by these thoughts" an extinct metaphor
even my 4th graders then put lots of chainsaws in their writings
and have the family die if they get tired of the sentences
one even made the lizard into a giant rainforest superhero
"so the animals and rubber plants won't be haunted by us."

letter to a logue
left to mono-
head high above in the center of a rope bridge
lists of things between the lines:

ticket unpunched
death registration
atomic bomb in a list with "cashiers for mathematics"
always the other way
systems of things fishing
measurement
weapon to combat
language
scissors
white produces black because of its whiteness
how a child defines
poems only happen
when you share in the making
even now we can never answer

Dear Danny:

Hello. too   I've   touch   and   apologize.   you   are
sicker   in   of   anguish.   I   powerless   you   but
least   love   genius   wit   heartedness.   no   one   met
36years   humor   quick   hesitate   insignificant   know   in
hence   pretend   even   clue   sweeping   your   body   What
do   be   you?   drive   see   with   Betty.   tears   for   be
of   healing.   like   used   oils   feel   up   it?   matters
crossing   path   naive   to   see   again.

Yesterday saved a fish's life
stole a sea gull's meal
learning to live all over again
the true scene of children and that
"digging in the sand gesture"

Carousel

On the blue gulf, do you see a fin rising? Roosters with tulip lips, a horse frozen mid-stride, legs curled, nostrils flared. Mirrors show them in parts, a body on time. Fatness as a way of speaking leaves you hungry, not knowing words without capture.

You finally figure they lied. She levitates over the table, spins while they avert eyes, pretend not to see. Walking away from water is a form of mourning. Her body ships itself feet first out the door, starved for air.

H.T. to Susan Smith Nash

Outside, a steel heart beats for girls riding roosters and wild horses. Defined through resistance, you may become what you resist, nothing else known. Row, row your boat gently down. Full of fear like everyone else dying. Cruising the trench. It's dark and there are no real names.

Red lights flash the carousel against night. A mechanical monkey plays. The girls, encircled by straps, post on their mounts. Water stripes, gull child. You watch from a table at the Yum-Yum House, drinking coffee. Straw hat, velvet streamers, legs clasping the horse. Never take your eyes away, being a beholder, bringing yourself to be held.

Organ song for boys shrieking on the Laser. Smell of french fries, coffee, hot dogs. That circle of lights in the dark is Stonehenge under glass, beside a frog pond, watercress fringe. Horses still stop there to drink. Inside the spring house, radishes and yams, the freshness of sharp roots. On the loop-de-loop, she sees black and dies. Nightwood for swimming into irresistible scenes among cattails. The small white back of a child climbs into a black car. A man drives her away.

On an empty stage grandmother sings "Some Enchanted Evening" while the child taps it out in patent leathers. In a porcelain and stainless steel kitchen, they bake silver cakes with mocha cream. She sits on a high white stool, surrounded by custards, sausages, flounders. Grandmother's turbaned head hides baby-thin hair, her skin glistens with orange skin cream, her room smells of April Violets. The child hides under a bed, eating chocolates purchased with her whole allowance and reading *Shackleton's Valiant Voyage*. When the music stops, you stop spinning on that horse but remembering who you were, can't climb down.

Repeating as a form of homage to ancestry: conjugation subjugates nerve, verbally agreed to mean nothing you want after her. He reveals himself at the door when she doesn't even know her own secrets. The red leash, sandbox in twilight, radio voice top of the fire escape, always listening, dreaming monkeys.

When he does it again and again, bleating fields, down caves and highways, when she stops worrying about form and lets it happen, the monkeys make sorrowful noises. Still she goes to meet him, Ezra Pound doing Chinese translations, entering the garden at night in a cloud of smoke, a hat with the brim down close over his eyes, fish swimming too close to see.

Once she showed herself, a clear wall of waves washed her out, back into her mother's mouth. Morning air, lemongrass, blue heron, treasure to win back, swim any stroke to slake that thirst.

Ball toss in the silver goblet for an ostrich ballerina or a troll. Toss this hoop in the rubber monster's mouth. Gun down advancing alligators—"now I'm really mad," the carousel circling. You are so amused you sit back while girls full of purr run naked through night alleys, return smelling of fish, follow fat gulls, whale songs. This is what it sounds like under water, mother.

Angels in the ministry of grace, defend us. Hamlet, Act 1, Scene 4

This hugging the edge where waves shimmer and foam is not the cruel center or the place where there is no center. If you hug the edge which is the idea of circling, the truth has no image, no face. Image as a form of surface, free. Circus freeze. Circus freex. His favorite line was, everybody remember where we parked.

At The Mall

She bites off the price tag before she speaks.
She leaves unsaid the obvious—her compulsion
to hurt herself may be the finish of her.
A woman with gold sand-dollar earrings
glues pennies to her glitter-painted sweat shirt.
I hear my own voice turn into an old canvas sail,
tearing and shredding in a stiff gale.
My backpack is concealed in the plantings
so I can sit here as if I carried no baggage.
She does not manage appearances so well.
Her hands are chapped, not by inclement weather
but by holding on too tight. Her eyes are lifelines
attached to nothing. Her voice drowns
in the sound of the wishing well fountain.

Susan Smith Nash to Lisa Houston

Venice in Furs

She lies on the beach in a modest 50s swimsuit,
a beauty baking under the gaze of men smoking pipes,
fanning themselves with leaves from rubber trees.
My sandals stripe the daylight shadows,
her inevitable death by water.
I think this is prosody imposed on the moment.

Her lips.
The history of a body
predetermined by the body itself.
The scars anticipate the injury.
The injury self-fulfilling
the prophecy of scars.
Mother's Day.

Good tubes to surf the body's regrets,
sand-patterned volleyballs for eyes,
gulls & terns that look Pacific.
She fashioned dialectic
in a Victorian giftshop
to front the margins of Cape May.

The falls at the edge of the cliff
rumble themselves blue with waiting.

Caves, no doubt due to their hollows,
mimic narrative before causality was inserted.

The House Codex
from *fragments for navigation*

i.

a squash we associate this with chiding   leave it undone
the little certainty of: certainty being cheap   he calls out in
his sleep when   he is   e-mailed   folktale

for amusement   this usually done in the bedroom or in
a gaze like what comes through the screen door: Nothing
certain as the hand that patting the blanket   far away what is
under his hunger

has fallen several times today   the narrative being
in winter by chance the light coming in yellow yellow—
meaning is not really swimming

in a regional accent the houses
of faxed paragraph we snap away and shelve   only this:
we say we are

reflected by instamatic taken somewhere while
chaperoning the body   in the morning the letters
of words called out to the baby
the soundbite we just heard another rhetoric
reread   the heart of a people

insistent   electronic choices tell underneath
it all or not at all or purposely ignored

in the kitchen with the water running

Lisa Houston

ii.

eight a.m. cuts your every breath   these cries he
does not like to be dressed by

language   has his own now which is quickly assimilating   can sigh

but can also pull himself up

            ∧

sitting in the shine of five o'clock   he knows
every plank will map it out

           /Λ\

his geography's truth compels me I am
pushing the icon out the sleeve

          /ΛΛ\

invented wings for amusement   laughed at
the potential for liberation

          /ΛΛΛ\

no perfume worn in order to avoid
mistakes

          /ΛΛΛΛ\

tossed on the blanket
these *santos* fit inside his fist
to put the mouth to

          /ΛΛΛΛΛ\

each life, then, being a degree of
gravity   much like the candle lit occasionally
so as to be seen from the road

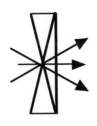

Lee Ann Brown

Katie Yates

Spring Ulmer

Deep Gossip Not

The whole shifts	the world that is
written specifically	every remembered
for the chain	sequel

elegantly pursued

something called	or not deep gossip
" " is lost	no separation my
or just misplaced	fixity italicized

I can't sleep

to splice	moving or doing it
or be that way	slowly be clear
is my question	an able architecture

our nonexistent wedding

still writing	finds a terse
"is it happening" or	love still too
it is happening	abstract isn't it

but won't play or	forgetting how to
shut Death away	deep gossip not

Amana Girl in Black Winter Coat

Amana Girl in Black Winter Coat
Amana Girl in Red Winter Coat
Black Print
Bleeding Heart #2
Caballos in Celo
Fall
Figura
For an eye an eye i
Self-Portrait
Soy y Luna
Spring
Suicidas 3
Winter

touch
girl   and your cheeks

         (an ice caught
         fox)
    are sallow,

our resemblance isn't
fortelling of
        how you don't fit
        only my
    sorry body

sorry the slow tart
sorry the bubble wine
sorry the fishermen kissing
sorry the florescent michigan
sorry the tadpoles lay eggs
sorry the small girl went home
sorry I then invited attachment
sorry the house is on stilts
sorry it's cold
sorry there is only one place heart
sorry there are many paces heart
sorry the come and go lovely heart
sorry the tender finger lifting sucher heart
sorry the terrified fraction of second heart
sorry the milkman touching the bell heart

sorry the father having married the daughter heart
sorry the elephant having mated the bladderwort
sorry the plant stalk makes lather heart
sorry

is relentless
of being equaling killing of

.

Abigail Child

Gail Scott

Two Countries

Bodies coexist in motion

The Sun low over Upjohn Chemical

•

The field has more yellow
is sink white, bright white, iridescent
under a sky formed regionally and in jerks

> *in perfect disagreement with the dictates of*
> *War*

•

> *In order to entirely satisfy, something must be*
> *evaded*

•

Bombing scenarios on TV mark the failure of the physical

The trees have shadows, empirical stripes
massy, insistent

•

> *still fresh, still climbing*

•

A 'wet-dick party' is how he described it

•

roping vowels
on a double
incline

•

Pushing the shape

rapid blossoming
light, against the background of stars
and movement of planets

drawn from the ears, tongue-tied,
snack-footed snow swept once
and patterned wastes of high volcanos on a cycle platform

•

I admit it's difficult. The lines are more numerous
They intersect less and less often and further

wobbling stun
pedal initiative

From us than we thought

•

as if ,
the month of days could make carved rocks conditional

•

A victim of the sum
unreconciled midst mutual technology

•

Everything sweats
The colors go even. The light pales
The colors disappear. Everyone is huge

•

and then we meet
a *norteamericano* "who knows how to do things"

•

So big he had a room for me to decorate

•

I defend my antagonist

T-shirt reads: *lick it suck it slam it*
and on the reverse a price list

16 billion   33 billion   300 billion
contaminates
washed up

from *Carwash Cenote*

•

A body bag ends the list of oil products

•

this landscape salty, poorer,
occupied

Worker semiplex Worker pictures
underemployed Worker

•

Can you make sense of this future?

•

Wanting the biograph to be a first step in serial composition,
subject to hybridization

•

slaves and honey *miel de abejas*
beneath a "fierce" sun

•

The man as objectified muscle tames the beast of burden
She rides the glamorously exotic circus elephant

> *We get a canned version of some mass that remains unnamed*
> *because there's too much break-up in this system*

•

Extinguished night starts again
lacunae exist.
   see: wetness

•

shadows heave irregular flowers

The empty and pockmarked.
The perfectly sporty
A Mayan nose *biologically*

Living beings hold together

•

A man annihilated in black rains of flesh

True men are made from coincident beds

Become laminated, crumpled, crushed, prised loose

Which is correct?

•

a más cerca al ultimo, tiene más calor

head whacks in reverse
Coca-Cola canned between lagoons

•

somewhat loosened
looking impressed
and roughened
by money

•

vistas speak of a high-level conquest
enlarging the supporting mound

•

sun rakes stairs with handles of limestone

ticking time
shallow
reedy
burgeoning

•

heat
under shadow of ruin

•

A plan with built-in excavations

•

All the work in a sentence.

•

The pronoun matters only when excluded

•

In parenthesis
unfolding breaker mimes earth in movement

•

The present and past irradiate each other
Sky keeps time
enormous foam

•

sea-tossed
in the margins

(stoney)

•

The clouds are Hollywood
The foolish tourists sit in skulls surround
the backs of slaves on which a regal

                leader stands

        on the backs of slaves

                •

        and we stand under

                •

conquest with collateral distance

(as seen on TV)

                •

(permissible) in the act of blood-letting

'Taking' more to the point

Greed, and a kind of impossibly hard cruel horrifically
snouted façade

                •

        has fleshless jaws

                •

        and his enemy 'death'

        collapsed bone

•

When smoke clears, disturbances are forwarded.
They form a double ululation
festooned across an inner ear

•

marked in figures
consumed in transport

•

Land invaded to leave no part of it in
light

•

Infected occluded globe
begun again against an axis made

fist

raw
uneven

The Sky is What I Want

An Excerpt from *Main Brides*

Lydia sits, her feet (in shoes with straps) planted firmly on the floor. Noting several chairs, oak-stained, only slightly more substantial than "kitchen," are empty. Nearly time to hit the road. Above them on the wall a MOLSON sign half-blinking so all you see is "MOI." The "MOI" reminding her of Z.'s ultimate withdrawal into a kind of egotism, i.e. a strong identifying narrative—including speaking only French—in order to gain confidence. Not that Lydia blames her. Because fragmented-type personae permit intruders, stepping in and operating secondary spaces of control. Full-time or occasionally. Like that fake-cheerful mother's voice being interviewed on the radio from her kitchen (likely green) in Verdun. After they found her daughter's body in the park. The mother saying she never knew how to reach her—but her daughter would call up, saying in her cute and peppy voice: "Hi, Mo-om. Everything's all right."

"Ev-ery-thing's all-right," mimes a meteorologist on the radio (slightly French accent). Speaking of the heat wave that's been going on for months. "*E-very-thing is normal, un-til proven o-therwise.*"

"Une Stella Artois," Lydia calls to the waitress: the new one passing by her table, touching, now, her shoulder and making her feel good. Lydia smiles, thinking: "I could grow old in this place." Where people are always touching and laughing it up like crazy. She means the Portuguese guys at the far end of the bar, gently sparring. Or that older couple of intellectuals, the woman a little stout with wire-rimmed glasses, sitting at a table reading European newspapers, comfortable and happy. Lydia imagines them in some café in Lisbon. Maybe the café on the cliff by the gateway to the Alfama. Looking down on the bay, which shines absolute gold at dusk. Later: full of twinkling lights of ships as if the water were the sky.

"Plus a brandy chaser," she adds, partly to be nice. Partly because she hasn't entirely sobered up and doesn't want to either. Not that she minds returning to her empty room. (Fake fireplace. No phone. Formica-covered kitchen.) More real at a distance, as at the end of a telescope.

After this, she'll go—

She gazes, pleased, at her domain. Taking in the throbbing dance music, under which (unfortunately) an anxious voice is rising:

" . . . so *depressed*, I couldn't stand the air. Had to step out to take a breath. Then you ask someone for help and they say: 'Oh, no, sir, I have to go to the bank. Come back later.' And you come back and they're gone. It's fine to drive around in a new car and look elegant. But you have to think of others. If you make them feel bad, they end up so depressed . . . "

"Distance," she repeats glancing quickly out. Knowing that under the invisible stars' high, dizzying arc, the long ever-narrowing street's still climbing towards where the sun set earlier. Lined with closed storefronts. Dark glass, signalling the importance of obliqueness: i.e., a *thing* can reflect a multitude of others. Like a gesture in a photo, pointing outside the frame. Or History, if told through constellations of signs or images. Example: History told through smell (since smell's the Queen of senses). She thinks of the "brides" she's inventing, now partying on the roof across the street. If kissed on the nape, the telling odours they'd emit. Nanette slightly lemon; Adele of Halifax violet; the woman who went to Cuba, sandalwood; Z., herbal yet rigorously exotic; Ivory for the dyke from the West. Some of them are dancing behind the fake Turkish domes, swag-trimmed cornices with pointy spears, or finials, on the corners, jabbing at the sky. And down below, the bar, slightly in a lull while people wolf down odours of grilled chicken, fries, rice, beer, smoke, cold mussels in vinegary peppery sauce, fish and sauerkraut.

Her own scent is musk.

She takes out her mirror. To see how "musk" translates into image: something slightly animal. Thinking (the mirror's slightly foggy), one of these days, she'll do a portrait of Herself (the past not dangerous or nostalgic if telescoped by the present). Maybe something kind of Cubist, held together by her present knowledge of the subject. Say, at the point she moved farther east in order to change her ways. Fasting, translating (just a little). Walking. Cutting every contact, except the magic of the Inuit. Himself more cut off than her.

The music throbs harder.

"The guilt of self-assertion," shouts a woman two tables over, puffing on a cigarette, "is like the guilt of doing art."

Lydia lights up too (although her stomach's queasy), thinking, "on the contrary, a woman can create herself from nothing." Example: fasting as an antidote to drinking (she'll start again tomorrow). Growing slimmer (then blowing up, then growing slim again). Until as sleek as Z. Lydia puts away her mirror, feeling for a minute that the best part in Z.'s portrait was looking out and seeing the men across the street with their ladder. Walking up and down. Then putting up the sign. Which projection outward gave Lydia (she didn't know why) a huge rush of relief.

She slowly sips her brandy.

"He thinks I'm beautiful," says a voice (soft Latin accent).

"What a stroke of luck!" (voice of friend, possibly ironic).

"But it's so hard living up to that. All my energy's gone. I just want to crash out exhausted. Is this reality or what?"

Lydia sips some more. Wondering if "reality" comprises what's just gone by in the mind, or what's in the process of unfolding. Wondering how this might apply to History. Outside on the sidewalk—some kind of dealer, and his clients. "*African*," says someone. "Your narrative's racist," says another. Plus various other discourses morcelled in the air: the meaning of perversion ("an apricot-flavoured prick," a voice suggests hopefully); or of "Canadian" (answer unclear), safe sex, serial killers. The parade of fashion going by the window, ever more chaotic, signifying the end of an era. Farther along in the dark, two women coming towards each other like dancers: same sensuality; love. Desperation. Two guys sitting down behind her. One, round and confident, saying to his friend (thin, dreadknots, features so tense his face lines are blue):

"Il s'est fait déporter."

"Mais c'est pas juste à cause de toi c'est certain."

She sits very still (the clock says 11:25). Registering how (also feeling nauseous) a few halogen spots brighten the tops of patrons' heads. A song called *Co-caine* starting on the radio. Reminding her, for some reason, that her problem with reality is that (like her grandfather) she is a philosopher of sorts. Always wanting (seeing) something more. As when he used to look at pictures of her boyfriends and tell her based on something in their faces, everything about them.

"C'était donc un Indien?" a Québécoise asked her once.

"Non, *méditerranéen*."

That's all about her background that she intends to reveal.

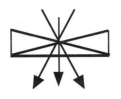

Norma Cole

Laura Moriarty

Abigail Child

Contrafact: *for Chain*

turned into surfaces known as luck
a kind of contrafacture with one foot still in the air
chain—containment and restraint
unable to describe it in terms of other shapes

"In its passage through thought, through words, every memory
appears like a sickness of language." Edmond Jabès
lines describing her complete arrival
via Santorini, dated "today"

the key stood up
there would be ships
amazed and what they see
something borrowed like time

something you were eating
(do you enjoy the city as you once did?)
the single overall deception
that tends to foreground those aspects

of your own life, "hair parted straight over"
look at the unreadable color
melon de Charente and then a toast
Elissa becomes Dido:

"I will give you all the territory covered by this skin." She cuts
the skin in strips and lays them end to end, containing the port,
the hill, the land around the hill.

Norma Cole to Laura Moriarty

each folded fact

"But I think the fact of years of love and the sure knowledge of
it is the thing that would make the most difference to the
person when the presence of everything goes away."
Laura Moriarty

three glasses just in case "for reading"
how the address structures your attention
an elegy lives underground
when something is not automatic

all eyes are not upon you
photographs of vessels, coins
how these exchanges take place
over the sound of water

like originals the translations were tortured
they got there directly or through an intermediary
"île de la dualité"
commerce, the green of English peas

shell beads carved to look like teeth
more crushing than torn
moving faces called masks
cavities into which objects might be cast

still think in terms of six shots
swimming through the forest
taken up by the desire for sequence
walking towards the dancing school

stores, roads, walking towards the xxx's
figures wear sweaters over their faces
no one is disguised, "flattened in fear"
flashing transgression, "hell to pay anyway"

accidentally, quietly an open door to other shards
no sidewalks, just *gutters*
"Gutters?"
working around the time of the explanation

the scale of time
one more working silence
"adoncs parra-l parlamens fis" Jaufre Rudel
in just this way the faithful conversation comes to pass

the prisoner's dilemma in ideological terms
cause is wielding their idiom transparent as threat
upper cabinet in back first shelf, bookshelf, greenish box, glasses
(car) where the keys hang

an inflammation of the eye which recurs
become a continuance of that mourning
blue burning ground
like portraits of strangers

(we do it together)
apple-green gold blend with the color of leeks
the heart is a literal qualifier
we hiked, swam, drank from the glacier, read each other's palm

inchworms dropped out of trees
faced in discretion
a base built up
false parallels drank in color

some refuse the work of reading
you look down at your hands and they are not yours
without attribution, word wants time
people are being bitten

"It's really sunny today, or, it's really raining today, these are
words people say." Cole Brager

it was a season
elimination qualifies

Triumph

These plant epiphanies
This residence underneath
Stemmed and read
Hands held out
Someone at this feast

Is dead already
Is not
Me with no meaning
Is not love
Is

Leaving life behind
Red on my hands crushed
Seeds loosely red
Read on my chest and heart
Dark

No longer
No drama presented
No law of silence
Needed
She was the secret

Laura Moriarty to Abigail Child

In this place he was
Event without article
Not a personal god
Went off with her
Without content

A stagehand carries a mirror through. It's supposed to be hell
but is just the neighborhood. A crew is here full of the illusions
of their story. We can't know them. Neither I, wandering,
lanterns suspended inappropriately above me, or you, freshly
dead, would care to know. Only later can one see them, only
not them, but the absent performers. It will be a false memory
pieced together. If time stops pounding the ears like a heart
loose in the body for a moment while we watch, it will be a
success. "The triumph of death" we might call it in spite of its
real name. So we can call it out.

Through the window
Not falling but thrown
With sudden force
The household
Out

Tables stained chairs torn and
Wobbling anyway taken
By strangers in trucks
Used up
Lamps broken notebooks

Ink smeared
Face like the stain
Of ashes ashes on the roof
Of course this tomb
Is a house

This airless metal
Number burned circle
Doused and scattered
Plain granite
Hell is heaven is home

This goddamned leaking sieve of a pen like a slow detonation.
If I could just get the right dress I could get it off me. Go back
and keep it from exploding. The pool of saliva that was left like
a last clear thought. Tip of the hat. Final handshake shaken
repeatedly. Spit like acid. A solid lake in a terrain which can be
picked up and examined. The world as model of the world.
Life as ending. The sun on my table burning as I fall, as I wake
up.

It goes without saying
I loved you more than god
"I am cancer. I am death."
Neither of us wrote that
The face wrapped

The eyes gone
Stuck at the beginning
A mask clings to your face like an animal
An ordinary thing like laughter
Sleeps here

In a dream my reader tears open my stomach the better to read
and I think, "Good, I'm finally dead or asleep and am cheerful
because change is the only way I can tell time now." In fact, I
am laughing because I don't know what else to do with my
breath. There is so much of it. All I know. What's here is there.
Keeping up with the air.

With hidden noise
Black leather and glass
Brushed every day like teeth
Fresh widow unfastened
Reading is breathing

Necrorealism

On the walls of buildings were proclamations: "What does
the red star signify?" Because he can spin a yarn with such

suspense, such innuendoes. And then there opened up
before me the gates of a universe which I scarcely dare

dream about. Oh, come on. The weather is good to stand in
line. If history is to be creative, to anticipate a possible future

without denying the past, it should, I believe, emphasize new
possibilities by disclosing those hidden episodes of the past

when even if in brief flashes people showed their ability
to resist, to join together, occasionally to win. If the order

is reversed, a different pattern is observed. Being as blunt as I
can. Then deliberately she put out the light in her eyes, but

it was still there on her lips—glimmered against her will
in her faintly susceptible smile. Silently, daring not to breathe.

The official figure was slavish, unabled, a muffled-up man
being crushed. From Monday to Friday, from the beginning

of May to the end of July. Upon his return from Siberian
exile (in early 1900) Lenin was forbidden to live in St.

Petersburg, Moscow and all the industrial and university
centers of Russia. At first her reading made no progress.

•

An occurrence that is an *accident* versus a
deluge. To substitute one thing for another.
To intoxicate and suggest—the essential
method of the fiction film approximates it to
a religious influence, and makes it possible
after a certain time to keep a man in a
permanent state of over-excited
unconsciousness. *Full of beauty and
convincing realism*. The revolution started
  on Sunday, January 9th 1905, with a
peaceful march of the workers of Saint
Petersburg (more than 140,000 people) to the
Winter Palace (Excursion number 3). *As if
listening to the explosions above him*. Who
made an eruption into her apartment and
smothered her with smacking Russian kisses.
Eating your past—
  a kind of necrorealism. *My own wardrobe
isn't large*, Lenin used to say. Her charm was
in that particular combination of manly,
young man's ways—I would even say her
male businesslike air with the extreme
lyricalness, maidenliness, girlishness of her
features and outlines. There are drawbacks to
these optical
  amalgamations. *Better to be the hammer than
the nail* says Tanya. In 1973, construction of
five-story walk-ups, which but ten years
earlier had accounted for 82% of all the
housing built was discontinued.

•

It is *normal*, by which she means non-explosive. We adapt to
'reflect' reality. From the edge of the Moika I turned

into the field of Mars. The unblacked-out windows of the
house on the corner attracted me. There is no prose without
past, present and future.

I
                                    would keep catching the
car
in the act of being recklessly sheathed,   while
the land   scape   itself
went through a complex system   of motion,
the daytime moon   stubbornly
                         keeping abreast
              of one's head,   the distant
meadows   opening
                         fanwise,
the near trees   sweeping
        upon invisible swings
toward the track,   a parallel
rail line
all at once   committing suicide
       by anastomosis,   a
bank
       of nictitating grass   rising
                         rising rising

----

1. The Soviet authorities would not even consider recouping the huge
investments in housing through rents, which have remained at the 1928
level.
2. I was probably incapable of expressing his version of indifference—a
monumental tapestry, corrugated and ruined.
3. I visualize her by proxy as she stands in the middle of the station platform
where she has just alighted, and vainly my envoy offers her an arm she
cannot see.
4. Once past these, there were only halls with plywood partitions and a series
of stoves under separate bulbs, one of which burned in heat, pointing to the
second floor and drying sheets.
5. For many reasons, by the 1760's the baroque style was gradually ousted by
classicism.
6. There is of course no actual connection between the two, but the
repetition is characteristic.

•

With a sudden turnabout of his whole body (although it is
strange to say his whole
body

Seeing how very little that whole was and how very much
it was not a body)
Directing at me the whole bird of his body.

Now write a dictation (having just done something else).
Very lovely, very lonesome.
Already walking.

The Neva is a comparatively young river, no more than 2500
years old. Even his skull, with that inexhaustible energy of
growth that was hard

to call hair, was physically perceptible as the surface of the
earth's sphere.
Which in spring burst forth with abundance, ground carpeted

in white violets, cuckoo birds crowning birches, ice
on the beaches. But what am I doing in this dreamland?
Somewhere, or other anywhere

From somewhere or other, from anywhere
when sometime or other,
somehow, some way (or other) (in) any way.

We use the present tense in the dependent clause
—even though the meaning clearly
is future.

Now,
the colored pencils in action.
Now,
Aelita at the foot of the escalator.
Now,
clouds in the sky swim in the vast blue emptiness and meet in so many combats and duels that, if I could only snatch a tiny part to put into books or films, I would not have lived on this earth in vain nor have given annoyance to my superiors.

That twist was only the natural extension of that head, its innate completion and outer limit.

(Supplementary information about the comparative)

The consultants watched over what was "reflected." He is thus compelled to fulfill the duties of a whipper-in, as well as those of conductor, instructor and superintendent.

There's a certain level of frustration blemished by glaring failure.

A queue for nothing.

A cast of stupid lips.

As a child of the symbolist epoch, as the epoch's heroine, what could be more important to her than the color of her eyes? Pulling a flap of the jacket toward me, happy that I've found a wordless diverting occupation. *So much the better my dear.* The newest picture looks as if it had come on screen reversed.

Tina Darragh

Beth Joselow

may to meet the road you rise

We were going to a poetry reading in a sort of 21st century
tram that also was my grandmother's house. P. had his work
in a blue cardboard binder marked

V

E

L

off center, but I hadn't brought anything with me and I was
getting nervous. As we went around a bend, my poem
appeared in the aisle. Two rounded hills of grooved pavement
were topped by words and parts of words highlighted in yellow
marker. There was a definite zigzag pattern to the highlighting
which I counted (7 15 8 15 8 15 7) before reading the poem
aloud. It was well received although no one was there. I felt
prepared, and we went to the reading in an old school gym.
The other poets were sitting on the bottom rung of the
bleachers with the school's coaches. P. walked up, his hair a
stark white Afro parted in the middle and wide on the sides. I
was thinking how much he looked like Dr. Zorba, only with a
tan, when one of the poets swooned into the arms of two
coaches and started screaming about P.'s hair. That didn't bother
P., who read, then walked off, pleased with his work.

When I woke, I realized that the aisle poem was a lopped-off version of the Irish blessing. ("May the road rise to meet you..." etc.)

lessing
ise to meet you
our back
rm on your face
r fields
l we meet again
is hand

Tina, I said,

Starting out, we were on a staircase that wound round the circumference of Dupont Circle, our daily commute to our jobs in the peanut butter factory. How had this come about? The question of endurance had not yet entered our minds; we were simply pleased to have others beside us, dishing out food for thought while we rose.

This road became the gone thing when its obligations turned off the corner in a foxtrot, became the occasion of discovery. "To rediscover the ancient hearth, to revive the fire in the midst of all these ashes." Then we were on a personal journey, begun when the Major smashed the crystal vase, declaring he was not the father.

The train rattled round the bend, accidentally dropping some of its cargo, including a series of sealed love letters written who knows when. Above the clouds, a gold thread wove an alphabet through the atmosphere, wrote cirrus, stratus in golden wisps of smoke, dust, steam, revealing the presence of countless moving, charged particles.

I could not count them, so gathered the children yet another time to point out a scene they may not have noticed in their eagerness to get to the end. My arms around their shoulders, I said, "It's the picture of all pictures that most needs an interpreter," then left them there at the long window, already starting to chatter with excitement.

Finally, we entered our minds, gathered above the clouds accidentally dropping a staircase through smoke, dust, steam. My arms wound round the circumference of the ancient hearth. The crystal vase, revealing the presence of all pictures, including a series of sealed love begun while we rose, simply pleased the occasion, these ashes.

Beth Joselow

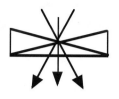

Stacy Doris

Kim Rosenfield

Joan Retallack

Heists:

A Long Island mansion, lynx in the hand
found dead, the mind out, wouldn' let her quit

so little human, becoming a gun

on metal shell pried
to switch back home – in slacks

all that litter—humph.

Wait a sec.

*hot place

I am wearing

Remember

too much pollution

Some swimmers

pastimes ease through

more   hills   to   push

some sharp crawl.

★

So much beautiful—
it doesn't matter   things

to spend

is worth something

Kim Rosenfield to Joan Retallack

9/29/93

She is wearing
    (the) mind in side out

on *parole* (colon)

Oh yes yes (I) was tran sported

the erroars of Medieval times become the language of Romance

among my dog's pleasures:
      to get very hot (lying in the sun)
then
      to get very cool

Judith Goldman

Lee Ann Brown

Lisa Jarnot

Sianne Ngai

Renga

February 9, 1994
Chinese New Year's Eve

discipline is not   Goldman
angular it has its cracks
and longer shadows

       sizing down a snow–linked line   Brown
       Kodachrome green framing on

an angular it   Jarnot
has failed the strange and longer
cage of winter it

       it's linked to bars without gloves   Ngai
       a finger's inner study

if links in the frame   Goldman
fail lines, fail color give in
to winter and stay

       stuck on words for the New Year   Brown
       a disc of snow on the mat

where asking it is   Jarnot
stuck to whether over it
is strange and that for

       narcissus fails, it asking   Ngai
       without scent, without winter's

consent or presence   Goldman
between bars and over frames
lacerate the disc

        seismicity fingers   Brown
        a pattern on the rough

in presence without   Jarnot
whether winter's outside in
selling inner in—

        the whether fails and that the   Jarnot
        bars are over for narcissus

or phrase, you describe   Ngai
it's music whether without
the failure is scent

        which is never written out   Goldman
        the phrase comes in asking where

angles upright since   Brown
the orange is bright next to my
phone calls in the book

        where in Spain the phrase is in   Jarnot
        the castle since and upright

less steep it spirals   Ngai
where absence without whether
is scent, orange bars

        are crevices between snow discs.   Goldman
        Spain heard phone calls in a scent.

Jessica Grim

Jean Day

Jennifer Moxley

Kate Rushin

Untitled (for Chain series)

Being
    inspite   everyday
of who you keep   becoming along the edges
                   also
with no need   suspended
   reaching me the town
times itself
still equals the town

"I like things to mean a little more suddenly"

everything that happens
  in the shade   of the absence of you

quim river

same as that   vault
   bodies   adjacent

the bid always low

meager   emotional inflation
        regains
lovelier than anyone had remembered
and calm

promise you'll snap
       someday

more never than absolute

weary on the bridge
where you are always
        crossing

moments pass   into the pan

sanitize   go to books

        mortar

coming upon ourselves in the wilderness
it is serial, flawed

penumbra
        generates "camping"

                • • •

exactly like the land   creates
        my balcony
                less your balcony

damper under
graveyard in roadcut
        hence we do
        not impaired but writing
            kissing the side of my mouth

experienced only as fuel
        control
                daylight longitude
        homeopathy

  my sugar
buoyant   boy
  more at the side of the road
    to languish

junk sunset

about as much as when the world lights up

habits have smells

sequestering inspiration

          walking on the sky like the subtle
lowering and lifting of loneliness

halfway in the dark notes

                • • •

maybe at the thought—waiting for sound
      covered up
              still sucking
your tongue on my mind

not dark enough to begin to see
can you ever

it is too wild and hazy

          switch hero's for a heroine
      who's looking back
                  random love
forms' pulse   meandering

thoughtlessness becomes you
as does desire

moorings

it starts whereupon it starts it is
token

                • • •

          someday   a remnant

whimpers that I can
      taste you,
      love, microbe

glistened on our
       stunt tongue

nice arm   on you

pensive only to a point, amigo

       my development for you elapsed

my god but you've grown the
very vowels of your teeth shine and
turn in the glow
    marooned   igloo my time
is come

what is *Babylon*
wanton buzzer

ultimately only
      concepts that cling
      fetish   and lake

provincial at rear
dilatory   hubris

able-bodied decade tenses at
    thigh on thigh
unchanged in its excitement

comfortable clay of your face   breaks
      drama milk mother
feeder affronting
timbre

nearly toward you

so strange   in flight

carapace   intaglio

little, very little, then nothing at all

it could even have been your own arm

Coming upon ourselves impatient in the wilderness
everybody's got their maps.
On mine more is barging out
than in. Citizen flies
are reckless, the sudden (bra-less, extra!) note
means it's serial
the getting there or failure, a road
made newly
of smaller bits.
I employ a vehicular vernacular
but where to? Divides into what?
The long afternoon slides off into
subterfuge (her and their—an act) and horse hysteria gallops
after the non-voting clandestine elect
whose sovereignty
splits the vault
over the river
we may then descend
and still do. On the brink of an ocean
of thought, the pleasurable activity of the pronominal mind
laughs, makes salt
opening on a mouth
odd proposition
engineered to the exact specifications not only of speech but
popularity (the quiz of rejoinder)
exactly *like* the land but not it,
into which we say we'll never swim
then, certainly, paddle.

Our paperwork never ends,
rejoicing in the phenomena of vice
and versa.

What are these winged words
that have escaped the barrier
of your teeth?
   Nothing doing,
nor my fault the Ford
won't start and so
   as walked across
you become land,
    bedded be my wilderness
    bookish my landscape and sea
    a bridgeless head tease.
Would you deign me everyday
if nearly to you
I were to say: "hey,"
   would you find me
contemporary
if Aristide stood for options
betoken of banks on which
no pronomial carrier
can stand
or gaze upon singers sweetly singing? O Ramona . . .
    my ocean is sold
    my ships of steel
    and all my nuclear submarines have drifted.

A man on the corner
begs experience
as moments pass into the panhandler.
Were we the land's
before we were landed? And then suddenly

things meant homelessness,
               alas my youth disbanded
               asleep in the automatic
               teller machine booth
while all the while
you stepped up to carpet
and a brand-new skin product,
as sadly I am now comforted
by leather.   *brick upon brick . . .*
If Aristotle stood for option's well
               brick upon brick . . .
a skinhead with a lead pipe
in the conservatory,
               brick upon broken
neck, thanks to my skin
it only happens
in my shipwrecked sleep.

What are these winged words
that have escaped the barrier
of my teeth?
          Nothing doing,
an evasive act
as when the lights go up
and you no longer like
licking for me and the thing
becomes thoughtlessness,
                    lick upon lick
engineered, it's
autocratic eroticism, a person
to person phonecall
to my personal she-history whip.
          Whose sovereignty?
          surrounded by working
          papers and men my markings
a downtown trench
circled by suburbs and upwards
of one hundred stories
of sky.
It could even become our own arms race.

This is Not a Dangerous Poem

This poem will not spontaneously combust
or blow up in your face.
This poem will not grab you by the throat
and wrestle you to the ground.

This poem is not a laser.
It will not burn your retinas.
It will not leak, eat your flesh away
or give you cancer.

This poem will not lay you off
put you out, garner your wages
cut off your lights
or deny you coverage.

This poem will not look down its nose
because you have no degree.
This poem will not sneer
because you like pork.

This poem will not molest your children
or slap you down.
This poem will not drive by or
go knocking with a two by four.

Neither can this poem give birth,
raise the dead, heal the sick.
This poem can't turn gray skies blue.
This poem can't get next to you.

Kate Rushin

This poem will not pretend it doesn't see you.
This poem will not smile in your face then
saw away at your ankles
when you're not looking.

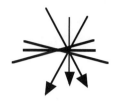

Lori Lubeski

Jennifer Hoff

The Collaborator

I stand by the King
even though his lost glove
is hard to find

the chain requires stamina
and infrequent trips to the
(archaic) bathroom

to be subtle you must
remain tortured
(from a distance)

when the mood shifts
to a more glamorous time period
wet will be the saliva
of the one made love to

and on certain days perhaps history
(unfolding into your hands)
will appear

★ ★ ★

What is blocked is the time
expected to have created distance
yet with this intimacy
there does not exist years

Lori Lubeski to Jennifer Hoff

(perhaps grooves,
   road signs
  to be full or empty
the gasoline smile of the
   long distance driver)

on our wedding night I expect to
be wearing the ring

yet his lost glove demands
our full attention

I remain devoted to
    grand larceny

★ ★ ★

As a duty to one's own (rural antagonism)

winter has now come and
come again
there is only the true duty
to the collaborator

     (I remember having come
     to your house late at night
     finding the man's shoes
     outside the window
     turning around instead of me)

no notion shows its belief
truer than these stories
more ruined by having
occurred than by having
been told

(She remembers my having

come to her house
late at night the shoes
outside her window
for fear)

Would be on your end of the frightened lease on life if you desired

the fragmentation brought about by such a sacrifice of paved roads

★ ★ ★

I still remember the gravity which was yours
the fleeing afterwards
a body more cynical than
what captured its attention

relaying a message to the
few who testified on
your behalf

        (You still remember the gravity
        which was yours
        the fleeing after
        a body more pleasurable
        than what had tempted it)

on a map appears in green rough texture of headlines

leading you into a more gleaming thoughtful landmark

And I am faithful to the collaborator
 at once your husband
who, finding the same shoes
outside your door
left instead

returns lately
still remembering
the gravity which
intruded upon
a series of risks

I am faithful to the King

        your beauty
        how many children
        were rough inside of you

        the commotion of DNA

I am partial to your behalf

in back history
glossy photos
appear grotesque

an everchanging
        agreement my duty

        is to
        what moves me.

Part 2 (The Reluctant Subject)

You are forced into collaborating with the one who chips your grandmother's fine china, making the tortured distance difficult to maintain. It's right there in your hands, has weight and is irrevocable. The girl in the story is there to keep a distance between me and foolishness; the boy is you plotting to hurt me; and the two of them are constantly ridiculing us and our moral postures, exchanging knowing glances with each other and rolling their eyes.

You are forced into collaborating with the past, and it is materialistic and self-satisfied. It loves the concrete object and all its hopelessness. It traverses a closed circumference, first scorning you mercilessly, then wanting you back.

Also with work schedules and train schedules. Because the ride is too short to bring you anywhere and if you miss your stop, you are forced to walk through the hospital district instead of the shopping district. There is no time to exercise; dressing well must serve to ward off disease. I am trying to localize my discomfort, *to administer a local*. The girl is making peace with the triangulation of truth with failure and forgiveness.

Because words and deeds cannot measure up. Because it would always be better to *see* color, a face, the ripple of animal skin thickly covered in fur. Better to feel your way out, even as the world becomes more like you and you become more of the world. Better even in the end to lose the battle and to lay down in the topsoil of the great Midwest after all.

You clean out your closet regularly, giving away the bad purchases and the no longer pleasing so that color and pattern will permit entry, interchange and betrayal. You picture yourself being photographed in a thick fog, your form barely distinguishable from the grey background of trees.

The boy and girl have little to say to us now and take to merely eavesdropping on our conversations. They become victims of superstition and witness many bad omens.

Maggie O'Sullivan

Denise Riley

Narrow Bandages Even Tombs

(In memorium ELLEN O'DONOVAN 1880 - 1945)

Now to the Ears

Having Journeyed to the Place of the
GIVERS

there is here

flicker.fleur.de.feather.fly.VOICINGS

on the shape
of storm novembers—

Double-bright & grief-iced

Rowan's
baited w/HARE'S

Amphibia

Crossings—

BEAK ON THE HIGH MOOR

Wastes
&
Flask
Fla Fla
&
i

wailed, wailed to the Peer of Liver Dance –
the Daints Choke

flicker –
sacrificial –

Crush Fo –
till.toll.tongue.me.sour
madders

Again thimbles, Again City, Again
hail on the ivy, i

Ones
w/the Brink
Engouled
Skull Brain
Boned Out
Mind Broke

be.al.di.di.
chats & thrushes
caca
configurations

Jexed
Axle,

Contrarian Dances

Shut/Air/Narrow/Bandages?
Should/Air/Even/Tombs?

8 other eyes in the lane white way towards the leaf dens

Poor Ones –

Convex Wires of the Crow –

Torched incalculably

Raven's finger –

Sets the Dog

the Rose of Air

jibbed out in the
name Again, Again

OUTLERED,

impenitent

WINTRA
SISTRA
SHELVERS
GROWLERS –

Hardly
the edge of it) –

UNSHIELDEDNESS

Snipe scream on the Bone /Breath
of the Blackbird

the waste of it

sob –
tick (ticca) –
told.te.me.

Don't Only Dance

shimmish?

December

Now the dark overcoats go slamming shut all round.
The rain.

And sparrows scraping under rusted leaves
The striped vines blackened and snarled.

Pitted grapefruit of the moon, peel off to a white furred pith!
And leave the dreamers of faces alone.

Moonface. To read the human onto everything
And loose a shower of syrup over zinc.

Being too many people, uselessly.
A whole day's words seep through the sponge head

Of the sleepless hearer, cell speakers puff and foam all night,
Press in on her the sheerest accident—that she

Is not squatting in caves, boiling up grass to feed my daughters
If I do not get shot in the fields, combing them for edible weeds

As here, there, the air
Shoves in to make swollen a space bled thin by any human going
   out.

White I cram through Shadwell Wapping and Rotherhithe
   blurred
Lights burning in the homes waiting.

Denise Riley

And I can let myself sag down onto the floor in a cascade
                           like a long curtain with a heavy hem
As also I continue to be held up

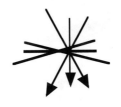

Kristin Prevallet

Elizabeth Willis

Electric seasons. Night has become as improbable as a sea forever at high tide. The sheer excess of light makes for a lack of depth, denying our fall from grace, the way a membrane is all surface. Or the way we, clamoring for sense, exclude so many unions of words from the sphere of language. As if one could fall off the edge of the earth. Why do we fear the dark as unavoidable defeat when it alone is constant, and we'd starve if it stopped watering the lawn of dreams.

Rosmarie Waldrop, from *Lawn of Excluded Middle*

Electric, ignite the surface
of tension. Between, a love
consumed by objects defeats
the impossibility of naming—
your appearance departing from the pier of limbs
sailing in search of greener seasons
is still a mystery to all of this, invisible body.

Improbable sea
green of my temporary
fading, into
tides that resist
the movement of moonlight
from a sky
consumed by airlessness
to a blue
that breathes.

Kristin Prevallet to Elizabeth Willis

226

Sheer sliver of our
shearing, together
this night
of silver
of light
will make dreams
of slipping
all the more likely
to sink into

Depth and falling through surfaces,
excessive beauty, you ignite me
ashes mark our ground
shears our blade
of grass. My entrance
to the roof
of your cathedral
is blocked
by the lawn
of your inevitable
green

When words unite us—
an enfolding
of syllables
and stars
spheres of exclusion
when what I need to say
in infinity
will you rush me
surround this my
ground, with speech
let me in him
never to return
whole

The edge of the earth
disappeared, swallowed hole,
and we are left
with blades
to sharpen
thickets that
we cannot see through
eye to eye

I fear the dark
defeated me
long before
you arrived
with the constant
of meticulous loving
that waters me whole
again the grass
is always greener
when dreams of flying
touch surfaces
not yet defeated
by fear

It's sweetness makes her lean with watered longing. And fear this globe that flees our touchy strings. A dusty clamor, constant in its exclusions, exaggerates unions with its dreams of defeat. When "the nature of woman" electrocutes this stony garden, the slope of her equation defies medication, and the greenness of prior thinking swims about her writing hand:

When I fear the darker syllables

Arriving at my temporary border
as if the night expected you

Again the grass of understanding
buckles to a meticulous obsolescence

discovered in our speechless seasons

Elizabeth Willis

Pam Rehm

Barbara Jordan

Monica Raymond

Catherine Draycott

1

It is often said that
              underlying diversity
Everything is One
              possessed intuition
The Doctrine of
        an Indeterminate Infinite
        holds us together

I have no wish to dispute
Heaven
it is only to be expected

We would have to confess
that the world has known little
of St. Francis

              The hands
              without a knowledge of the past

But we both know
words inherit
a military age

Everything is composed
              of Love or Attraction
              or Strife
this process continues
              without a stage

II

Impending thoughtfulness. The weight of it
sustained by a kind vicinity
where hundred-year-old linden boughs surround us
        in their calyx,
nobility of silence,
the far, blue umbilicus of sky. What can we
know, or find?   (The young St. Francis
in the dark, asking over and over,
My God and All, what are thou and what am I?
—there are many ways to ask it.)

But to make room for silence is difficult:
like letting a fire go out
in the dark when we fear the dark, and the leaves'
        soft agitations
become extensions of our own. . . .

3.

Two sopranos, a mezzo.

" ... they started on his basilica
before they even got through
the canonization, but he
was a shoo-in—a man
of the people, but not
the little people . . .

                    it was all
about clothes, his father made
his fortune in them, then when Francis
found his vocation, he stripped
before him, naked in the public square.

                    Then *he*
designed new vestments,
ones without sleeves."

Poignant pieties of *Ephemeral Folk Figures*'
scarecrow photo—undershirt (sleeveless)
slung on a crosspiece (headless)

or the snowman they say's
like St. Francis—eyes filberts, mouth
            a brazil nut,

when squirrels bash him, he
(literally) effaces, offers
himself to them

IV

In truth there were many falls.
The fall of the animals came with the birth of man.

Not one creature missed, golden haired Adam
Bound with names illsuited, each

Spiritless, stung struck Heaven, sounded *wrong*.
What concern was it of theirs

This tree, and the fruit Even sucked on
So splendidly according to plan?

We know words are too slippery, too irrelevant.
Shallow speech, an ordeal failed,

Made the perception of the serpent
A hypocritical twist to the infinite.

Only a real saint finds good in the guilt,
And in the monstrous, deep nature,

When wolves petition the moon manically,
Knows poetry, birthing the truth backwards.

Catherine Draycott

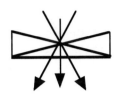

Joan Retallack

Tina Darragh

Diane Ward

Steinzas In Mediation

there are are there instances of this in every era
a new dispersal of the subject
or that there shall be a complete fragment
or that the fragment shall be
as if the is reflects is the
while is the place they were
between sometimes or what would begin in there here

I.
I And But That In
That But Whatever It And
They But That In Not
In All But Or Not
Made Made Lengthened But But
All Kindly
.

no the river hollow with I call them love
of up began from who who goes yellow
I must hedge whisper wet going over
straighten nothing to say un un in
glassed fill empty burn white

II.
It Or They Or Not
For They Because Coming For
Coming For Or Not But
As Just All All For

Joan Retallack to Tina Darragh

More Always Or Just It
As Liking It Once Nearly
In Who They Just Coming
Always Liking Which Mine Or
Often As Think And

.

of creating a usable past
in here's no where redistributive humor
how to not inscribe yourself in the system you're opposing
opposing opposable thumbs up to a point of no turn
not the turn to oppose to it at all

III.
It Yes As To Or
In Please What Not That
Not Coming He He Which
And That As Not Just
It Of She Not And
Or Not She When In
All Or For And

.

shades of images of and have read
instead s/he varied the speeds
synchronizing mind body as if
that were not a problem of no problem
were willing to leave blanks for to of what not known
no less with than 5 question marks 4 ifs no thens
I gave up Shelley after several years of living in Manhattan.

IV.
Just Or For Which They
It Or Not Nearly For
In All All For They
That In Why For In
That Should All For It
They It It While Should

For For Not No If
Like It But A And
She Did We After They
After Just Once   .

.

logic except for instance holding resembling
wake hold thing thought final hold dissolves holds hold
when word and lives the deep (70 kinds)
as if/no end/so botanist's eye exists
time sad power enor of off or at truant
the view like chinese poets some goat
west coast realtor sky green chairs rail against
altitude whats blur from more

V.
Why He All A Tell
Be Be It They In
Let They Better Not In
Not I Land Yes It
Might Did We Because He
Once How All But They
Once He

.

not to make a famous statement of about clarity
not to find the famous footprint
every third thought shall be my grace
writing synchronizing mind and bodys minds
one wants only clarity yet one wants truth (sic)

VI.
I If If He Namely
Often Left Come They For
Ours Made By In Made
Let But It Because They
Articles Hope Theirs Ever All
For It Just They They

They And With Getting For
It We WhoWith If
I Of As Not They
They That As Might Just
It This All Aimless She
That Well Or All They
I Gathered All Come See
See Shall

.

in description lies betrayal lies
in descriptions bounded in of or for
what we take as disolution and ruin para phrase
in this out or fall of for next generations to take for the or
a natural order of things
they will not seek their bearings or where we find ours

Stones/us   piece the middle

thunderstorm bleaching
orating air

trace:

rants of the face
ried and worked
nected ideas
Coade stone
cent ocean
plete orbit

_____

each cover
cloth in **v.i.** *knowledge*
overlapping in so
opposite toward LAP

_____

pack up be *pack*
measure *a*
is season

people tain *pack*
in floating a

a. therapeutic
the called roof

———————

pigment:
matter stick
as *as* describes winter
(something) or
Slang: of stops

nana which *blue*
human duced lips
See in the forces
square once discussion
fusely cajole < LL

———————

picket rier *outside*
within **Pale**
the sors vertical
encircle PEEL

shallow flaring
of mechanical ores
artifically hardpan
the (gravel
cize wash like
a fully resumed

———————

leafing numbers
them wristpin
ture the opponent
with *him/us* spalls

plumb pin now
haust closely *the glacier*
iary device

Mediate

I in regulate   not found there
issue of the conditioning
picture hand as an image
so aware the pauses there
ease   am I alone (here)

each brain wave is a bargain
please honey, lose the touch
settling on an image
like choosing the parameters of speech
the square with the wettest brink

a promise to adjust my situation
there there dicker dicker
all the time subject matters
elevates the pain to a level
profusion   saving face

the dot not easily conceived
tight concealment
whichever colony soothes you
and in this reproduction   alight
worn open, gazed upon

colloquy harmony self-consciously
soothe   a set of city images
paid in lip service   thirst
skid in excess   but to spend spend
inter-   using our squares and triangles to transmute

Diane Ward

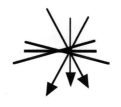

Phyllis Rosenzweig

Diane Ward

Wet

                                   wet places where
people wash, rinse and drain things
                                      the
                 touchy-touched body
                         the denial of the happy circulation
Body and someone else's body
                       The wedding dress symbolizes
sexual relationships
                the body is missing as if it had never
existed
                         Lynne:
                              Did I speak?
I think walking helps me to go straight
One knows, though one will never see it that this will never be
done
T-shirts make him sexy
                 Delicate designs
                 Find this detail
            human eye
the gallery for the Art of China
When I sleep I'm asleep
I love you
. . . his nightmare and the explanation of his nightmare
                                 Alejandro
Everything seems to be going well
                       The poor are hungry. They are
filthy. They are robbed.
You can't please everybody
They will hate you

Phyllis Rosenzweig to Diane Ward

                                        Between
            these two (you can picture it)
On the second bulletin board there is a photograph of
[a girl]
                They thought that what
                they were looking at was *theirs*. They felt
                at home. They thought that the
                place belonged to them.

Between

—two legs erase
dispatch in edibile black
white hiatus within each habitat
a monotonous de-sire, noncollaborative
to soak up drops from unconsciousness
I—frankly—muffed
creativity AND prosperity
the Bride and Her mechanism
have found leisure too taut to be of use
my twin subtle bodies
soundly moving ground

Body And Someone Else's Body

sexual, child-rearing and labor capacities
brief sketch with no greater ambition
was no physical object nor had it a real existence
taking flight and looking back
my heroine
who tried to be a portrait of the ongoing
the head and the heart
the silence of the real diagnosis
the silence within this revolution
spun one upon another
out-shaped and extended
location, without elation, too late

Delicate Designs

short hair for restricted sexuality
shaved head celibacy
I found follicles that mirrored
our attentive primates
I can't even finger the delete button
without thinking of you
its position and yours in this photograph
your thumb and forefinger, cliche
your filling the frame
within history, my comparable biology
learned not to blaze too broadly

Susan Schultz

R.M. Ernest

Carter McKenzie

Jennifer Arin

Sinister wisdom

If we knew answers, but not questions,
the sea might stand. If desire did not
precede its object, there could be no
objection to it. If the subject is dead,
then who are we to complain? Is there
solace in repetition? he asked, who'd
watched *Texas Chain Saw Massacre*
a dozen times. I wonder, averred
the logger, hooting at owls, feeling
his awls. The stage is set, I hear;
does that make it like a table? Or
has that motion been set aside?
It's terrible to see so many nouns
sit in as verbs, and vice versa; there
should be factories to make more—
free trade means more Spanish words,
but it's an easy language. She gave
it up to me, and I knew a border had
been crossed. It dissolved like
a mirage, or meringue on a space
heater. Distance is all in your head;
so are deserts. More words mean more
space, and that brings down property
costs: start the presses. No, not irons!
Are these sentences adequately creased?
He dresses well, don't you think, but
his vocabulary's such a drag. Not *in*
drag, you dummy! Not a dummy, either,

or donkey, even a dog barks up better
trees than you, my dear. You said the
chain mail's got you down? Feeling
like a knight that's past his prime?
My primer is prim, but chain link
fences leave out as much as they hold
in *Non sequitur,* I tell my students.
Little do they know of my secret life
as an anarchist of syntax, balancer
of budgets not my own, avid reader
of texts that'd put them under; she
rather likes grammar exercises, but
Gold's Gym has better rates. Steroids
or no, bodybuilders appear to me
repulsive; fear of flesh, or its
masquerade as metaphysics? Put it on
the shelf. There. Notre Dame *is*
a football team, I told myself in Paris.
As American as they come; we're all
hapa, really, even those of us not
computer generated. *Time's* always
behind the times. Sweet rhymes, dear
prince, and prithee stop snoring; the
bard thinks you a bird, parrot more
like. I love you and won't leave, said
the thinking parrot. We call it repetition
compulsion. Polly say that one! I must
to the broken tower go. Come see my CD's
sometime. We'll have some wine, and dark.

The Clutch

Step heavenly: you never
sausage a place or north
or south of the border.
Your own inflection
in the din of snowflakes,
laughing jags,
Black Beauty's white
whinny.

Muscle-bound for glory
the peasant under glass
is only sleeping.
Preterconscious one
can hook space flesh
tautologically construed,
points means as with needles.

By the acrobat's rat
o'nine tails which
when pulled, roots long
shear across wire
wound on a spindle
handle-cranked springs
backwards appearing to flow.

Subjects go, objects flung
like rice petals. Have
a nice trip. Come
close in controversy
who will make light
and marry music
confusing groom with clergy.

R.M. Ernest to Carter McKenzie

The Wedding

I couldn't see the lily of the valley
against the wall, the stone-touched light,
the way the priest forgot his stole
to bless our ring for joy of us. As if

against the wall, the stone and light were all
he whispered, "I'll be back" and turned
to bless our ring for joy of us in that small room
where I misstepped, grasped an overblown bouquet

designed to be a whisper, baby's breath, turning
for the flower lady, who frowned and rearranged my fingers.
Despite the misstep, I would pose for pictures, bloom
amidst the stone and light, well-groomed, but you

and I undid this flower business, nervous hands
that gave and wanted to take back. I looked
amidst the stone and light of us, the years
of our return, and whatever took us here

reached in, and held, and bound our hands.

Carter McKenzie to Jennifer Arin

Persephone

The walls here are black,
massive, impenetrable black,
uneven and rough
like the walls in a grotto or cave.

Skulls huddle in a heap.
Death is part of this closed tunnel.

Although I can barely see
slabs seem to weigh above me.

I study the walls.
For all their horror, they hold
a fascination:
these walls seem to shine.

How shine? There is no light!
No, but filaments of golden minerals sparkle,
spun through this underground black.

No darkness is pure, but integrated
with rays from eternal sources.

In this deepest shadow
I must survive
by seeing within:

Jennifer Arin

The spirit inside
holds his forehead to mine
and I feel there a golden sun,
a light, strong
as the glimmering walls.

With this, then, to illuminate
We prepare our return.

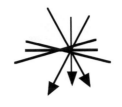

Cole Swensen

Elizabeth Robinson

Crowd

To love is to remove the face
Acres of day

God is a child who might
Break in a glance

Do it enough. Do it alone
Say you'll go on
Like this

When I woke up I saw a road
And realized I'd been dreaming
Of New York—not of the city
But of the name on a map such
Disparity. And then I woke up
And saw a face. It wasn't
A specific face

"I have been sad for a long time."
He practiced the line again and again
There is nowhere
In the world that doesn't appear
On a map

The magnifying glass
In its leather case
Still on the windowsill

One should never die with
The hands empty they should
Be full of hands. One should never let one

Cole Swensen to Elizabeth Robinson

And now something has happened to the throat

You must love God as you
Would a child. The hands so easily
Form a bowl and the face
In the water was no face
You knew

But we are changed so much by our bodies

And slowly turn the page

The water you hear running
Among this slow turning
Is something living
Where it can no longer breathe

You have to touch God just
Barely. The children playing
In the street are going blind
Bright flashes at the far edge
Of the cornea whole
At this speed

The heart is a machine

II

The heart is a measure a
Constant, count

The faces
Once
The gate of the face has been
Taken away

God is a fragile thing
That visits the body in fractured

Stories like maps of indivisible inhabitable
Territories like a child as you close the book says
Let's begin again

And now the heart cannot be
Found, blades
Of grass, a vagrant frame
You do but alone
And you aim

If the body were a country, a
Century and ice
The speaking made her sleepy
And she reached down not thinking
To take something up from the dirt
It was a doll's head it would fit
In your hand the face
Erased, the unknown face and the hunch
Of a shape that is the heart
That is a hive with its relentless community.

i.
Let's begin again.
A storybook
on a raft,

this unattributable gift
by comparison.

The black tabling surface
between the self and God

assumes the shape,
half a room over,
of a child.

Who would you love,
a child
or the possibility of conflicting lights

which offer rest?

Administer, they say,
a heaping teaspoonful, an antidote.

ii.
Some things about myself
I would be able to smell anywhere.

Elizabeth Robinson

The span between the table and
the wall

in the shape of a couple,
arms around each other.

God would divide the original cell
of twins,

these ones,

smelling the range of distances,

I would be one of two twins

who loves this image of God.

iii.
You hear water running
and the hunch of a shape.

Shape's intention as measurement:

and the domestic storybook shows
God baking a pie

so that when the oven door shuts,
its light goes out.

iv.
Would you love your alarm clock
which wakes you.

Would you love your twinned daughter.

I would love to read the story of
these vagabonds adrift on a raft,

so insubstantial,
who built a sink

aboard
so they could wash in seawater

and keep sanctity.

v.
Half way.

Lights so perturbed with each other
that they expand the presence of God.

Barely. The children playing
in the street are going blind.

These invocations are roughly
the same as sleep

disturbed again by the youngest.

From here to there an antidote.

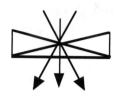

Fiona Templeton

Kathryn MacLeod

Susan Clark

b e Frank
l augh,   l   i e
l and D id   nt
   Par   t   end s
   If   we
A che   h e   R e
   in An ew   Rid e

Ba ck   in
Babe   Cha in
        G o   B e
Ba Re   r,
     t ha n
B   ra n,   o r
             Steel
B e Sh y.   B a
   s   ick
  anger   alters
  long Le a d
        Cha in
Be at   and
Be at   er   and
 l i ar
       Se   e Sta i n
    M at e   d
Black   to   win
B oom, He
     S   lips
   o r M y   o ne
  one   Cha in
   is H ard   Steel
Boy   C a n
    G orge,
    a ch
    Rob
    a ch
B ow Dar t   in
  own   gene,
        m ock
B   oy
    Me
      i   ll
      o   il
                   m e
Bur   n   Bald
   k ill   Ba d
   Donald   .

         ach e Move s
      B   y
 I n answer i
 p   a le   Fo   r
C r   e ator,   and
Car   e &   i
       Ca n

Ca l l   M y
           s on
Ca n Donald,   S ee
   a   W   a y
        ill
           D ie Fo r
Cha in   S ore
       Rid e
        n >   l a in
     as   w e
           t o   re
           Bald
Cla   lmer &
        Rid e
C e   ll   Rid e R
C li T   s a   d
Consume s Power
   No charge—   Enter
      G orge,
Coo L
   ou e is   a
Co   ld.   Rid e R
C   ar e   Col   d
   on   ha n d.
C   O v e   t
           tension r i sk It
           Center, C u t us
     i   ts
    ne A r   s ore
C an   He
Crin G e   ill
C e Ll   ill
Cross   s a ne
           S ee d
Cross   to   S ee
Cu t s   Le t
       R e d.

   a s   Rid e R
D   rank,
   ever   i
        B en   d
   ever   y,   Cha in
D   ea R
        B en   d
D   ea R
        Rid e R
D   rea   d   Pee
   in   m   y
    g er M s.
       So
   n o   Rid o
     g   r it   w e
     lay on
        lips t O   y
        t Rue R
Dru   n K

   m   ale   Ri   d

Early Art   i
   swor   e
       n one
   me   r e
       R e d
      Cli t   F e d
   s lr ing war

  a s avid S ee d
  a s Donald
Ever   C an

  arm s le t   a
Fa ce mes   s e d
F   e l.   Pee
Fe e   l
  Par   t   l y
     an old   S ee d
  i ki ck.
     od d   i y
  i mo Pe   on
Fin c H ard
     Fe c d
F   r   i g
F   r   i g
Fi ll o ld   S C a R
  o Donald i
   s o rt
     S a i d
  w e   C a n
  r e al   Me
Free th is
     Cha in
  i Will   w e d
  t he Be n   t k ey
Full   y   S ee
F
F   R   r   i g
   t n Violet,   Rid e R

  all i am   ha d
     Ju   St
  sper m
   Donald
Gaze   ah,
     more
G orge avid   S ee d.
G or e
     me
     hard   hol d
   n ic p Ric e
  i C ar e
   fr Aud   ee d
  d r y we   d
oldman
     Rid e s ore
oldman
     Rid
Good,   a   Huff
Good.

Good Ha d   a
     s o n
     He   R
Good   ha n d
   rich e r   and
Go t   we d
Got M y
     ha
Go ld o n   Bald
Gray Wa ter,   and
  re   lent Walter
     E n d
Green er, Lo n G,
   B ad   l y
Gross, F a r   up
Gross er   ha Rd
Guys   an d
  a Ch es.

   Art   C an
     w e   Rid e
H   i m
   B ad   l y
all   in All
   B en d.
  a nd C ar e
     C an
Ham k er   Huff
  a nd h is   Rid e
  a Mer e   Huff .
Hand y How   re d
H i s   F le d
H e -   Rid e
H is s ore
     C la d
Har D   and
Har m Cli t
     He   R
Haught y
     B en d
H es
     o l d.
  y es, Rich ,   B ad
  rich o n
     Fe e d.
He s a   Ga y
Hi s he e l a
     Rid e R
  o h Rein old   ha n d
  t ug s   Rid e R
Ho t
     F le d
  over M Ine ,
     me
  over o ne s Ta r e
Good,   and
ought   i
     M il d
How   ol d
Hug s L ie,
  de ard,   en d

a s P   Rid e
      o r Els e   P et
            us   e   d
oh   B l   e d
    ston e
      Ga y
    e   dge d
one Pa l E   Rid e
    f   o   n   d
      it   La y,
Ju st   La y

Donald
            St O le
    d   r y   B y
      y   es,   P et
      H ating   Service,
      P et
    t e   ll   S ee   d
Kin d   S eel d
    i s   ank,
      s ur e   we d
            La y   le d.
    l   ose   a
lick,   g et
          a
lick, T ry   W   ry
      fer vid
      Rid e R
  o r, J e   e R
      B l in d
    or Jam   li   d
on us oh .   Wicke d
on   e   Wicke d
    th   e   B ad
      o   ld
      Art

a   Da   R   e
a ro   Le
      F le   d.
    in M   a d
      Fo   n   d
      Al ert S ,   and
Lat   er   All
      hard,   and
      h as   a
Law, a   He   r o   .
Le e   Ch ,   i
Li   a   ck   a
Lie   F ed
      St ill 3t ak e
Li a r   le   d
      d u l y   R e d
      id   l y
      B ad
over, Har d,   B ad
Love   M il   d
Lover, Ro t   Me

Lover, o ld   Pee R
o nes ill,   an d
o nes Co o P ,
            and
    ne   e d   B l in d
v es Ma   n
    a F an

    i   ski M   F a ces
    Fc   r
    a sha   re
    a   g   C la d
      sc   or.   Ri^d e
      t   or n
Ma   Le
      Ga y
      Will
May   Al ert   R   e d
    a nd   n c
Ma   d Gene
May   Rob   m e
M ad,   M y ha i R
      My   ha   d
Me   t   and   Steel
    Cle an   la   id
            Cha in
      le a   s   h
        a i R
      D ug
    c am   e
M i r Ro r   Fe d
M u s   C l   d
    Qui t   Cliff
            n o
      i   S at l   ost
            so
    l ick   Fo l   d.
    i s Donald   B a d
    l I ving,   and
      hell, r Ea l
      He   r o
    t ell, How   Fe d
of t   en
      any,
M ore,   i
            S   a y
Mo re   s   I am
      ha n d
or Cha s   te R
    dar e   B en   d
      Cl u e   He l   d.

N o My   B e   d
      A cl   Col   d
Ne   ar
New n ames
N o,
      Ba   R
      He   Fa il   a
2nd t   ak e

ı.

a   ble P ote   nt as
W   a   St   e
a   y e a r   St O le
a   Hard   r   O le
c   an   t
        i
r   e s T   i
so   h i d
t   o   F e el

o   s How
           me
          so   rry   Cha in
o f   r   a r e
          Fe   d
fe Ver
        ha   Rd
o   r   s A ne
          S   a   y
s c   ar   R   e d
    Will   Rid e
k   ill   s on

P l e   a   d
P   arry
    ters   e
        B e   d
Pa   r   R y
      Me
        Har d   e R
Pa   le   S e e d
Pa   L l   S
      T   o   Col   d
   da   re S
      Me
      s   ure
i   Wan   t
Po o   i ha   t   e
        R u   d e
        C   as S t o   R ch
Say   a M
Pu s s   y   an d
Pu   s H y   an d
   am   le   d.

well, G o
and He   ha   d
a dor   e d
S   o B i   ee d
h id
      Br   O k e
S   o h   e   He l   d
     be   A t
     Ch i d
ch   e   a t   a n d
S hu t   Fr e e
S ul   k,   Pe t
c u   n t
She er   Huff
ho t
      id
Sim   P er,   Pe t
S   E e   an   d
m   o   an,
S   ame   Vi ce
lo t   h
   i C a   ll
   W   ar   y
m   y   Cha in
S h ames B e   d
mi   ne ,
m   y   ha n d
   de   ar B in d
      Do g s All
   r E a   Ch
      rest,
   de   a d
me   n
Some   wo   Men
Some   Vi e
Some   Jam   me
So   d   Som e
Some   La y   B   a   d.
Some   L e   an
Some   g et
      R   e d.
Some   Ma n   F le d
Some   ill
Some   hard
Some   C a n
Some   d   id
Some   W   e   d.
Some   Will
      So
So   Rid e
   In   a c Age
      ak ey
p   Art   Cha in
  g   ood,   B ad
   s har e Cha in
   n   ame   Cha in
t   ame

a   ng E   r   Fo l   d
   Ma   n   up
   d   og   ge d
eve   R
      s   li   t
      B ad   l y
      How   B ad
ne   ver
e nd   n   ee d.
      s   l am   S ce d
hard   on
      h in d
R ide   lock
Riddle   t Rue R
i   H   old   t   ill
i   G orge,
      even
i n   Wa ter,
        an   d
      s   Wi   m
     dar   kl y
i s Donald,
      so   s   ore
      end so

/S   a   F
        S eve k
            o   r   Stee R
S   ens e   a i R
ic e
            a S   k
S   a id
S   o   rry   and
S   hot   me
    sick   e   dge
Su   ck   t   ill
  lif   e   F ee   d
S t iff
    if   Fri g
  w   on T   k e
        W   a

        lo   s   e nice
            ha n   d.
T   Wic e
Th i   Rd
T o   on o
        W   ke
          M e   F   ey
    i   D r   a in
    as   be t
To   oward
      f   e   a   r
            one
T   ax   on   nce
  u   n D id   He   ck

        on   l y   B   i   d.

Va ine   r   w e
    n   u   rs   e
        R   e   d
    Wa   r
      1st   t O
Vau   n   t He l   d

Wa ke   S ee
    a   nice   B e   d.
          D   id
      Donald   win

Wa   r ... ,   end
Wa   r. Le t ,   id
    a   r M
              n one
W   no
Wa   i   ed   Rid e
    de   Ear   Me
W   E   T Me
We   G orge   Fo   r
We s T a y   ow e   d
    a   L   a i   d
        B   ar   B a
W   o n   ha n d.
        oh   C an
W   e   c ure a   vision of the
          s   or   est
He   o
W o o, o   r
          F   en   d
Wil   D   B ad
    l on er   o R
Wi s e   And
        Rid
        se   E   v e
      ro te   r est
      i   d   S ee
Wi t   in   a
    f   on d   Fo l   d
      s   a d   an   d
              Ga y
    l on   e   B   in   d
          is   Fo   r
Wor   D   s,
          and

Ye   s,   me

    i   r an
    i me an, i   C   an
        e   R y,
          He l   d.

Blessings

I.

After reading the text, I bled profusely. There is a way of looking at the whole mind and body, without subsets, without death, or clutter. This is in *her* honour.

Not everyone can be important. But out of the gradual disintegration of light, or matter,
comes hope.

Dear Hope
This is my new ship, my bullet train.
I want to speak each of your names
clearly and distinctly.
I carry my own dirty water, wash my hands and knees.
This is another way of meeting dreams.
Call it "a revolution in science." I remember
a face in pieces.
If I am alone, I am alone.

Their bloody closeness, a mixed blessing.

Kathryn MacLeod to Susan Clark

II.

When she spoke, her voice was new, uncertain—
as if she had not spoke before.
Committed to
authentic
"sex" cracked, bled
a small voice challenging
boy beside, inside her
the whole self
laughs, in pieces

Life approaches revolution
in a way I'd not imagined.
The patients run the hospital
doctors abandoned.
"We will fix it, fix it."
In complete sentences complete
with meaning.

I am surprised by my own
opaque context. Fear is far away
and intimate. Freud is resplendent, old, in his disguise.

To Wound, To Wind

By *good* I shall mean that which we
certainly know to be useful to us."
—Bertrand Russell

—ane, suf.
blot

The reader's blood
eyed the blood
on the page and
fell

a bag of bones with wings
hairs out of place
—someone's sight brought me

always devoting space
fishing upwards
down here
leer a leash
overtaken

as the road

its meager timeline, clothy

". . . holding up her own blood, even mentioning the material"

Susan Clark

275

ruthe *fr.*
tender pences
cf. lingual

A bit of brain'd
light was never

falling
falling mazed
mazed

amid their bread so cunningly held apart

—expressing clearly or obscurely the idea of a lower position,
the bleeding woman leaves and rejoins the production line; we talk—

Fronted distraction
particulars that litter
her specter bound

an opportune fury and a partial labour
—kind of dawdling
streaks of news made merry as if

An sluttish else
(weakened) ONE lit. to carry

hand closed around an abstract sensation
churns it self
a pelt agog

"I go to the grocery store and touch"
states want

a steep gist in nearness
mouthing a nil bale

                           semple, sourde

a floundering perfect cost
—whereas I'd intended mass

                       A tiny newness, stooped
and anyway they're eating it because it's dead past
caring for the past

He carries the amputated legs to be incinerated on foot
—I had no idea it'd turn out this way

            Glinting glasses for an event far from the head
            overtaken plump in a grassy break
            staining reflection

noon brooded on our guest.
her gag stuck in a box

This piece was begun as a word-by-word etymological and "in-kind" translation (including punctuation marks) of some of Kathryn M's "Blessings" informed by Fiona T's blockages/blanks, blarings-out and textual insubordination.

First unattributed quote (" . . . holding up her own blood . . . ") —Denise Riley

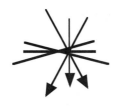

Elizabeth Willis

Julie Kalendek

Subject to like passions as we are
                    —Christina Rossetti

my soul herself, myself

a possession I could not

mistake for the man

(his language and latin)

yet we are "taken to"

a love passage

I had hardly noticed

in the late talk of money

The work of love and the work of art

has no sleeping part

is a drop of light

in a small silver socket,

a rosy dime

in a daylight tryst

is a *keeper and no spender*

as seeing him who is invisible:

a kind of flaxen thing

found in stone

I obeyed and read further

"I am hemmed"

broken,

your soul—mine
rained our scattered millions in
bad waters, this to him
auspicious delay, debility, desertion
the distance of a figurine believed
to be escaped or stolen
if then it speaks—
a scientific name for
crying in your sleep
or his hair strung from my things
what cost this fraction of affection
to be bitten at the heart
to make a fable of his shiftless stitch
a forgery of devotion
an outline in compulsion
perhaps a wreck of love
and then the work of art
It falls and we replace it
mark the unaccustomed fervor
as I stake it

Julie Kalendek

Tulsa Studies in Women's Literature

Edited by Holly A. Laird

Tulsa Studies in Women's Literature is a scholarly journal devoted to the study of the relations between women and writing of every period and in all languages. Publishing articles, notes, archival research, and reviews, *Tulsa Studies* seeks path-breaking literary, historicist, and theoretical work by both established and emerging scholars.

FORTHCOMING ESSAYS INCLUDE:

Forum:

ON COLLABORATIONS

"You Heard Her, You Ain't Blind":
Subversive Shifts in Zora Neale Hurston's
Their Eyes Were Watching God

Christine Levecq

The Long Distance Runner
(The Loneliness, Loveliness, Nunliness of)
Susan Leonardi

St. Virginia's Epistle to an English Gentleman, or,
Sex, Violence, and the Public Sphere in
Woolf's *Three Guineas*
Christine Froula

SPECIAL OFFER TO INDIVIDUALS AND INSTITUTIONS

First 11 years of *TSWL* (1982-1992) for $95

Offer includes domestic shipping; please write for overseas rates. Offer does not include "Feminist Issues in Literary Scholarship," Volume 3, Numbers1/2, which is available as a book from Indiana University Press.

☐ **Please send me the first 11 volumes of *TSWL*.**

SPECIAL OFFER TO NEW SUBSCRIBERS

TSWL is offering new subscribers a complimentary special issue of their choice.

☐ **Please begin my *TSWL* subscription and send me the following special issue:**

☐ South African Women Writing, Spring 1992   ☐ Redefining Marginality, Spring 1991

1 YEAR SUBSCRIPTION TO *TULSA STUDIES*

☐ Individuals-$12/$15* ☐ Institutions-$14/$16* ☐ Students-$10/$12*

*Outside United States   Enclose photocopy of student I.D.   Airmail surcharge: $6 per year.
Back Issue: $7 U.S. $8 elsewhere.

☐ **Please renew my *TSWL* subscription**

Name _____

Address _____

City _____ State _____ Zip _____

☐ Payment enclosed. ☐ Please send me an invoice.

Please fill out the above form and mail to: Subscriptions Manager, *Tulsa Studies in Women's Literature*,
The University of Tulsa, 600 South College Avenue, Tulsa, Oklahoma 74104-3189 Fax: (918)584-0623

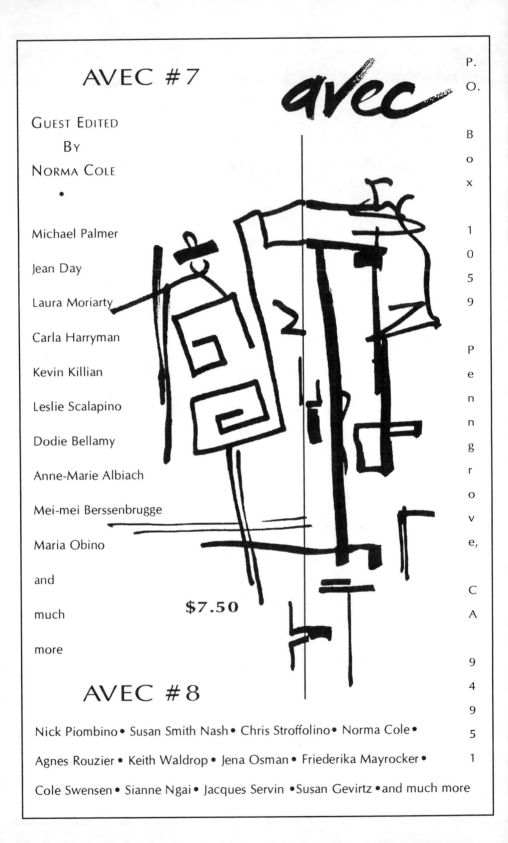

AVEC #7

avec

P.
O.
Box
10591
Penngrove,
CA
94951

$7.50

AVEC #8

CHAIN / 2

Call for Work

Special Topic: Documentary

In what ways does the topical world filter through the creative word? We are interested in sites of writing that address the definitions, limits, and practice of "documentary" through alternative forms. Essays, poetry, prose, and visual work in black and white will also be considered.

Variations on chain/chance generation and collaboration of work is VERY welcome.

Send submissions to:

Jena Osman
107 14th St.
Buffalo, NY 14213

Juliana Spahr
57 Livingston St.
Buffalo, NY 14213